HUMMINGBIRDS & THEIR FLOWERS

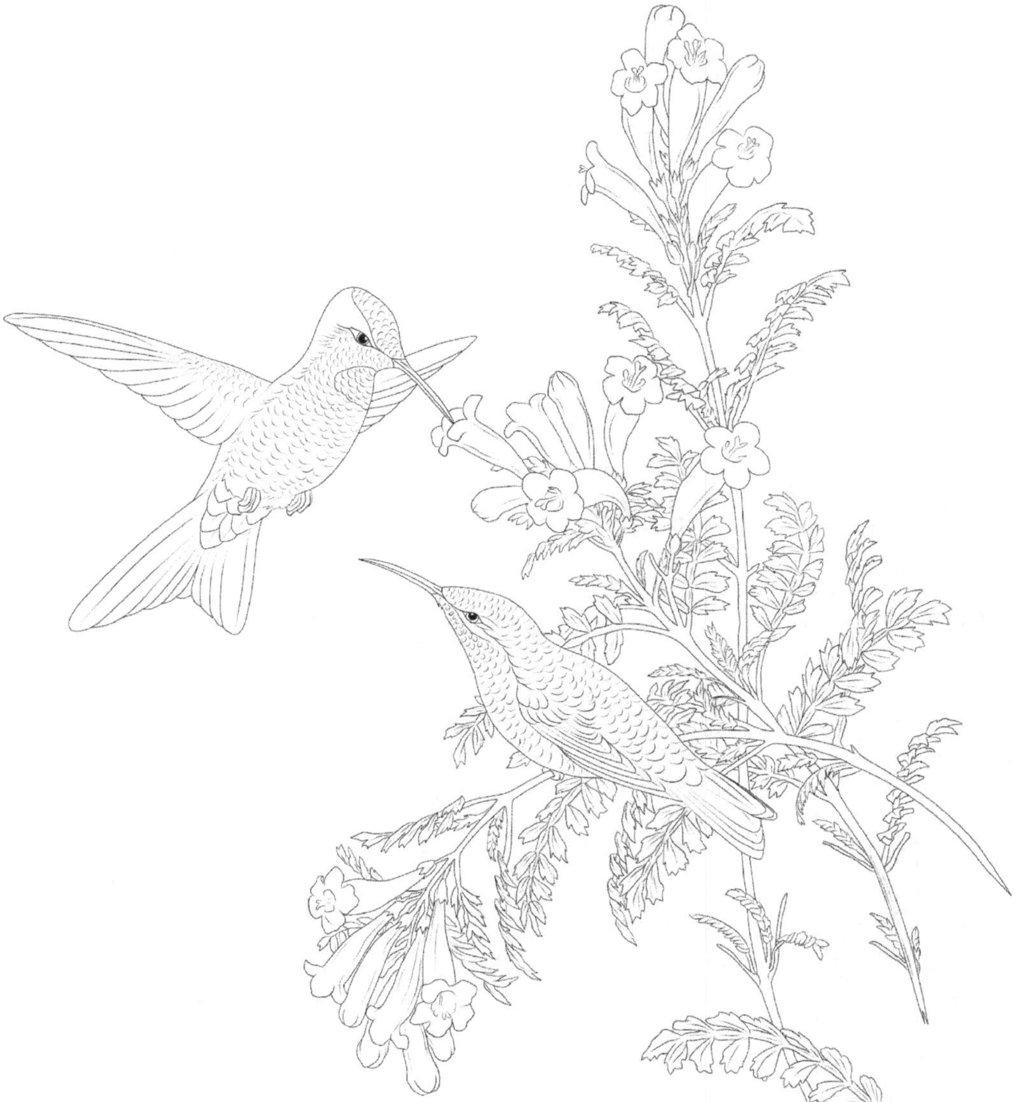

by Alice Balin

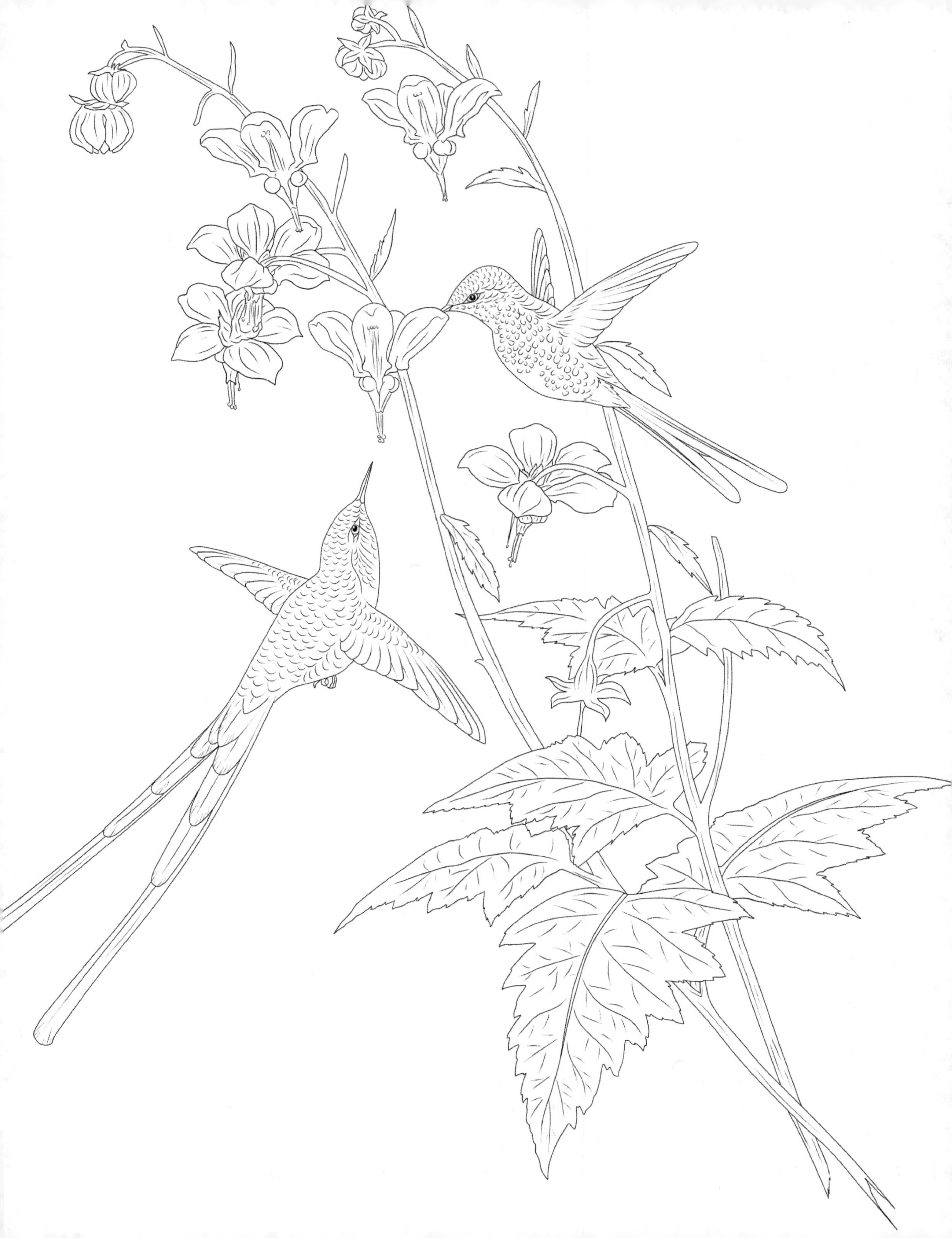

previous page: Graceful Train-bearer Hummingbird (Lesbia gracilis)
flower: Painted-flower Loasa (Loasa picta)

facing page: Green-tailed Sylph Hummingbird (Cynanthus smaragdicaudus)

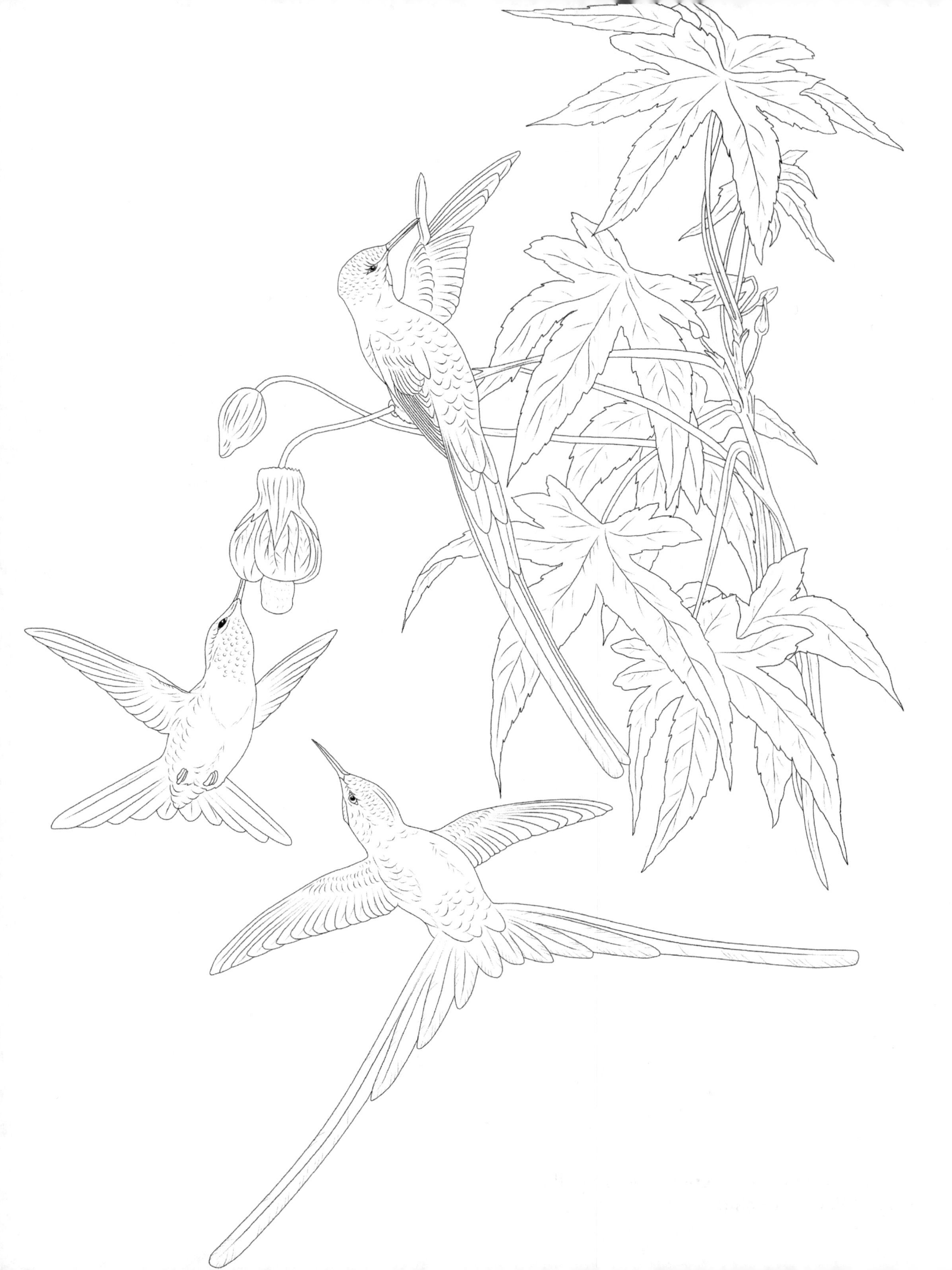

Crimson Topaz Hummingbird (Topaza pella)
flower: Miltonia Orchid

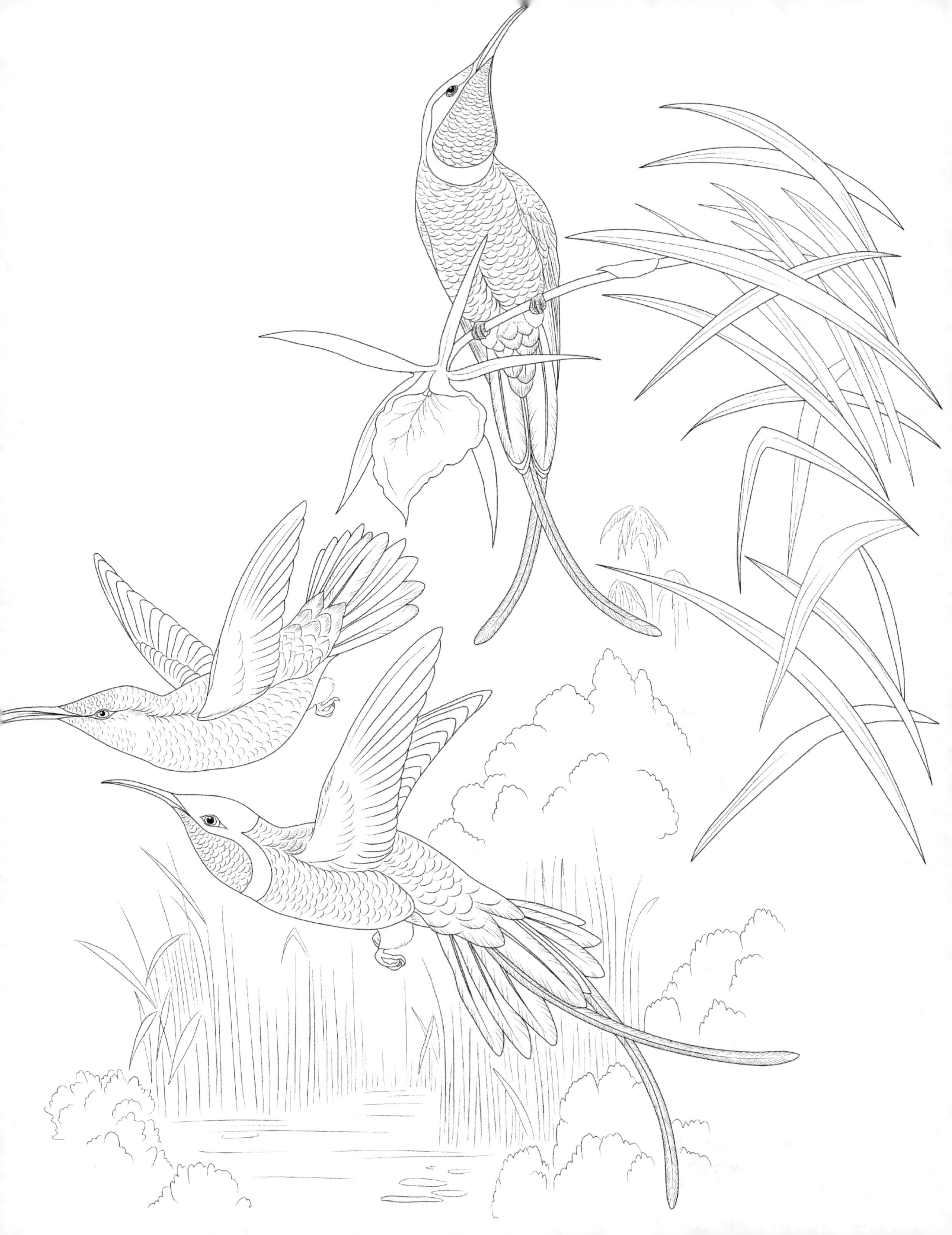

Green-crowned Brilliant Hummingbird (Heliodoxa jacula)
flower: Cattleya Maxima Orchid

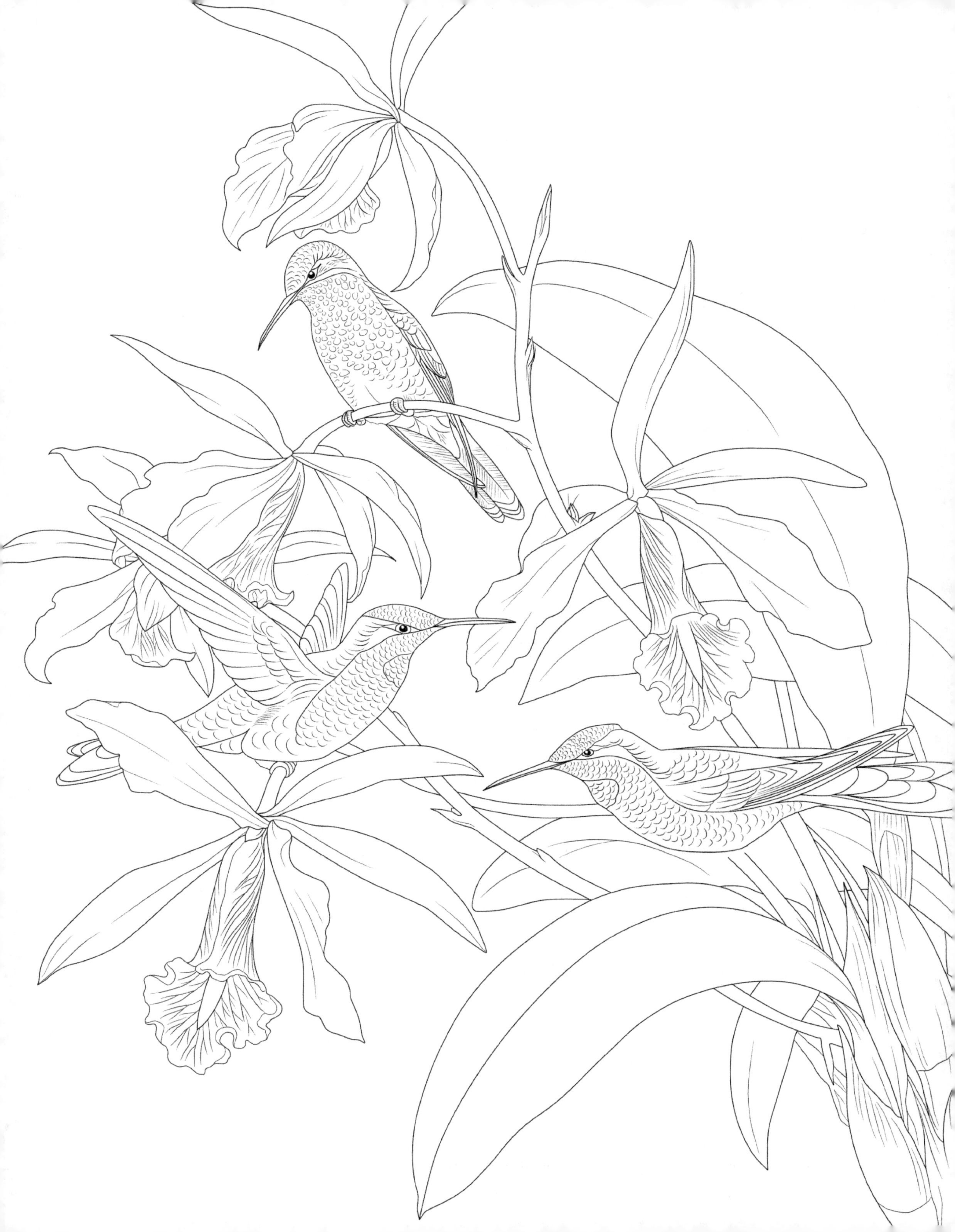

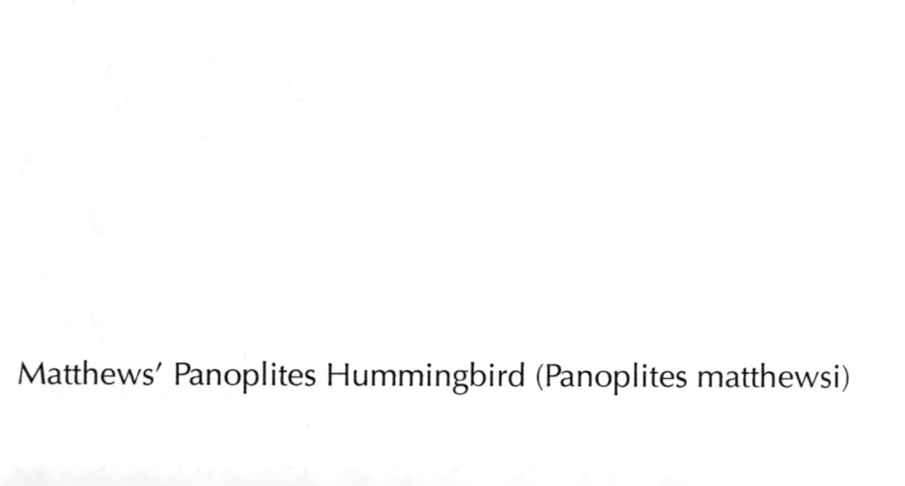

Matthews' Panoplites Hummingbird (*Panoplites matthewsi*)

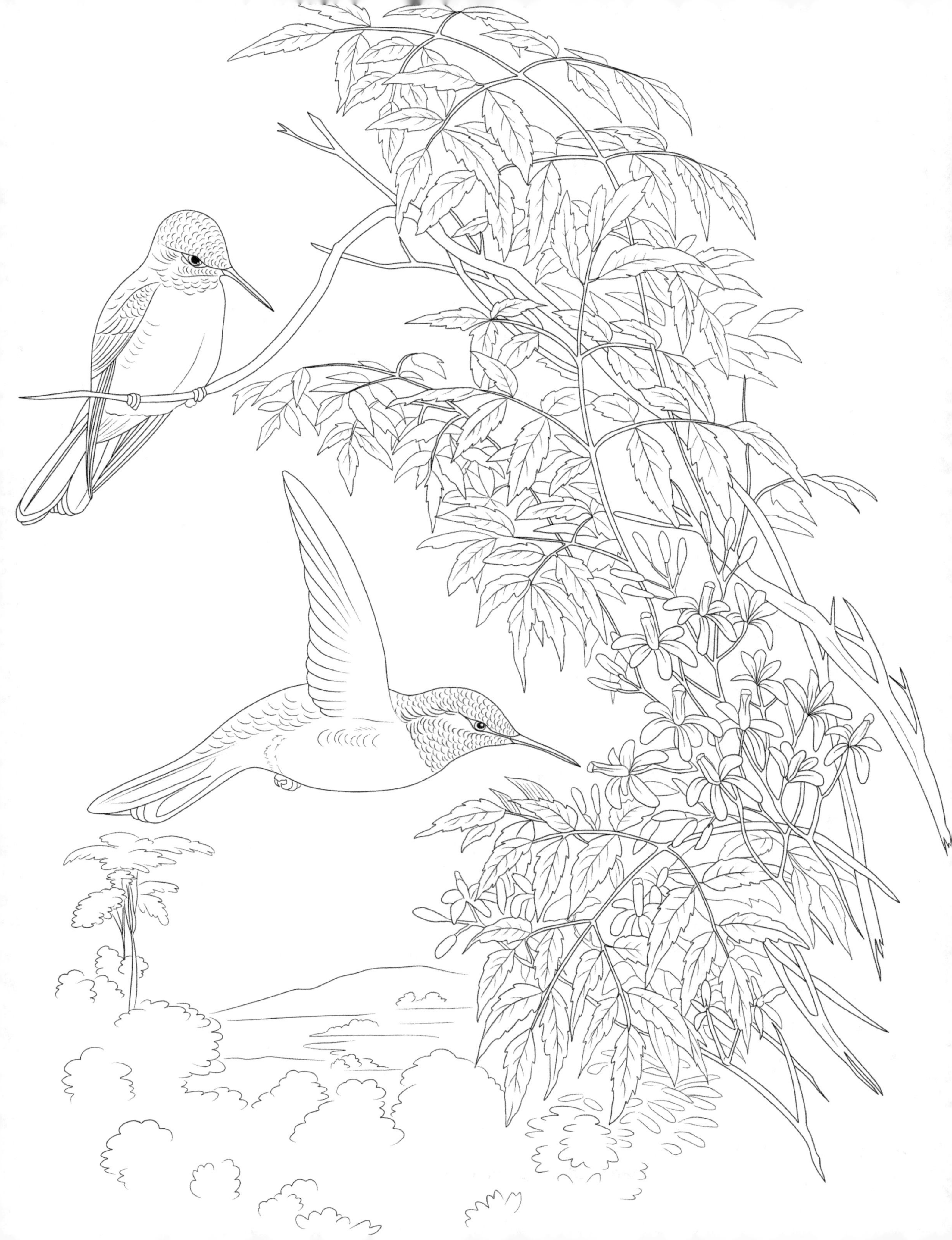

Nouna-Koali Hummingbird (Lesbia una)
flower: Cinnabar-flowered Elephant's Ear (Begonia cinnabarina)

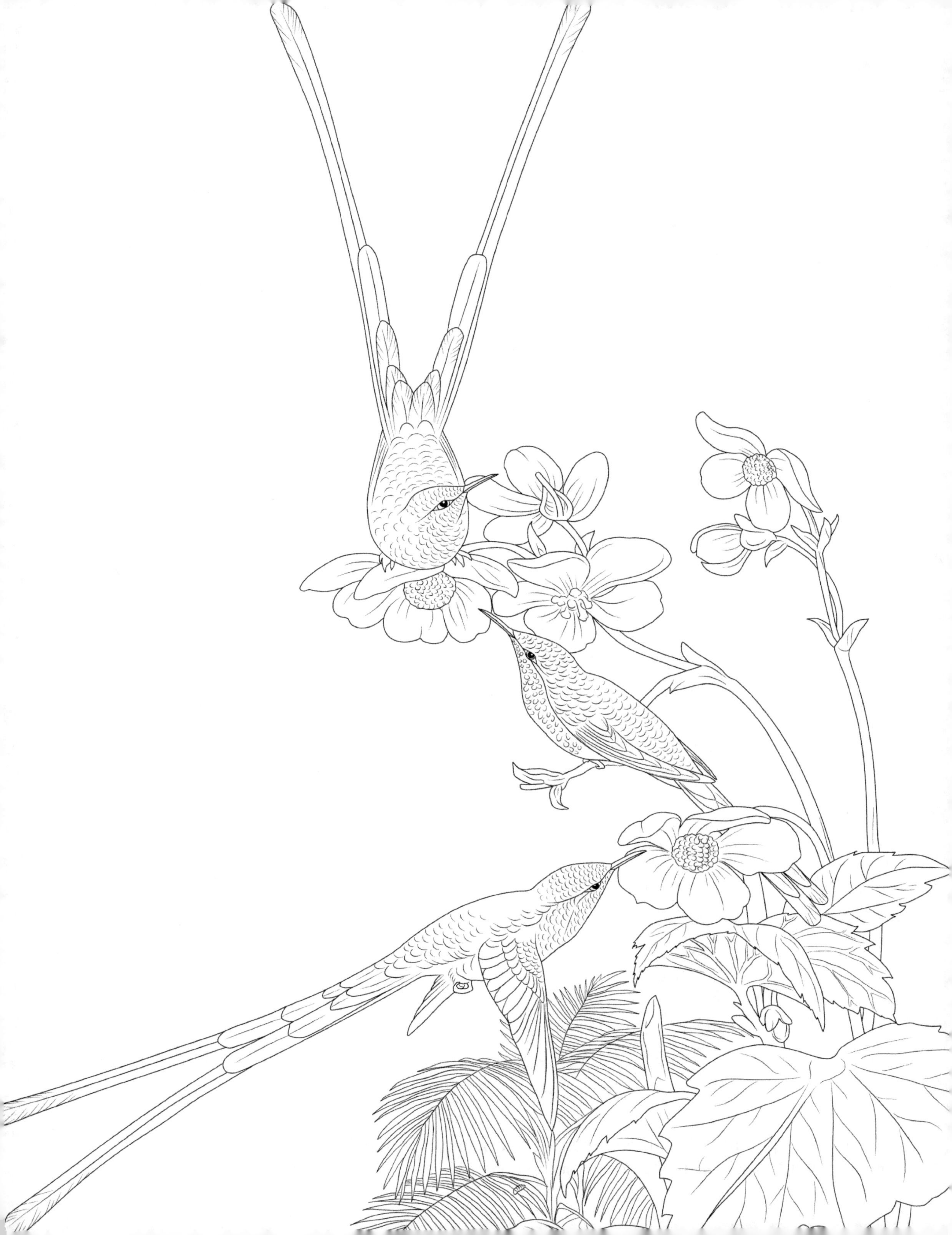

Temminck's Sapphire-wing Hummingbird (Pterophanes temmincki)
flower: Banana Passionfruit (Tacsonia mollissima)

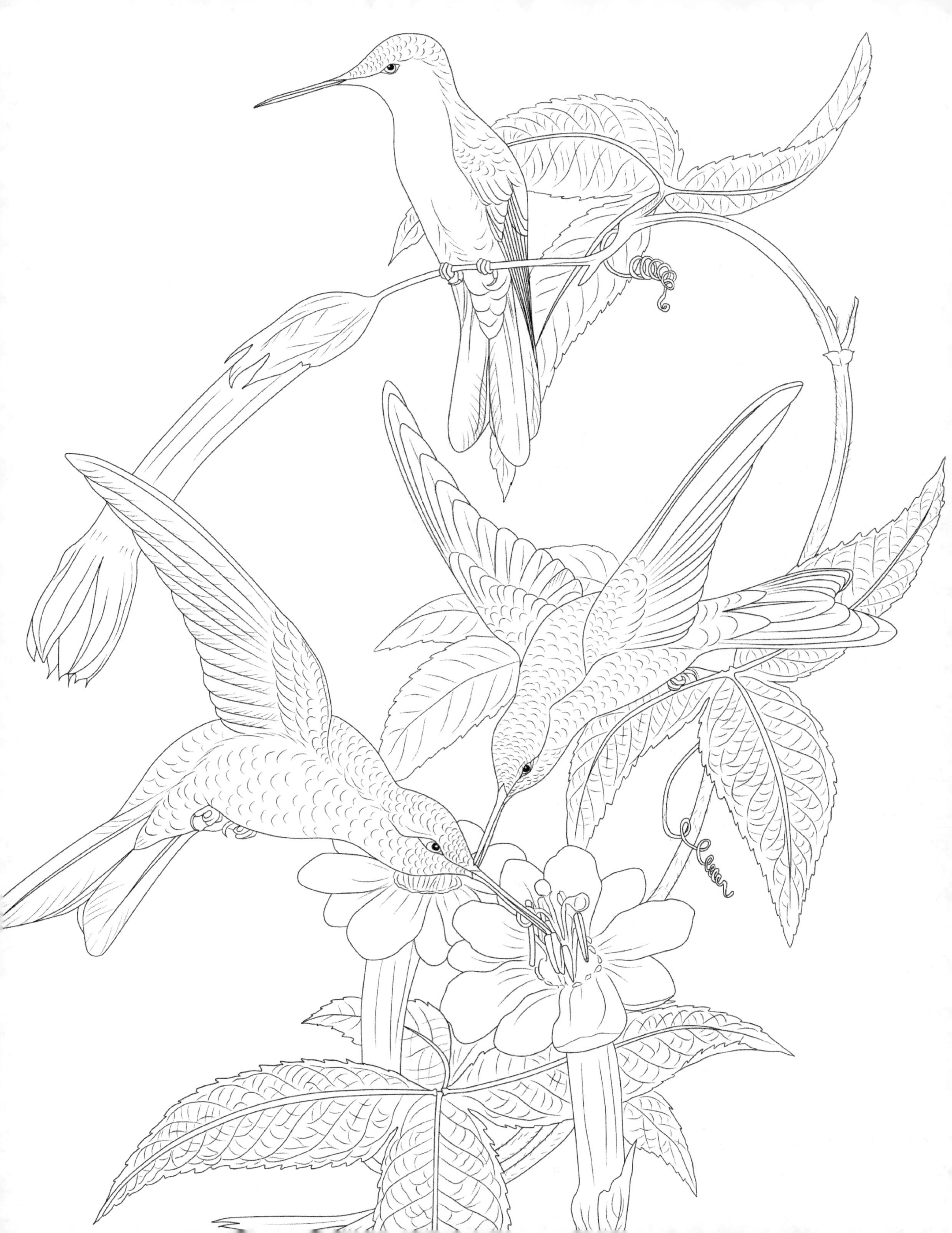

Glowing Puff-leg Hummingbird (Eriocnemis vestitus)
flower: Easter Lily Cactus (Echinopsis cristata)

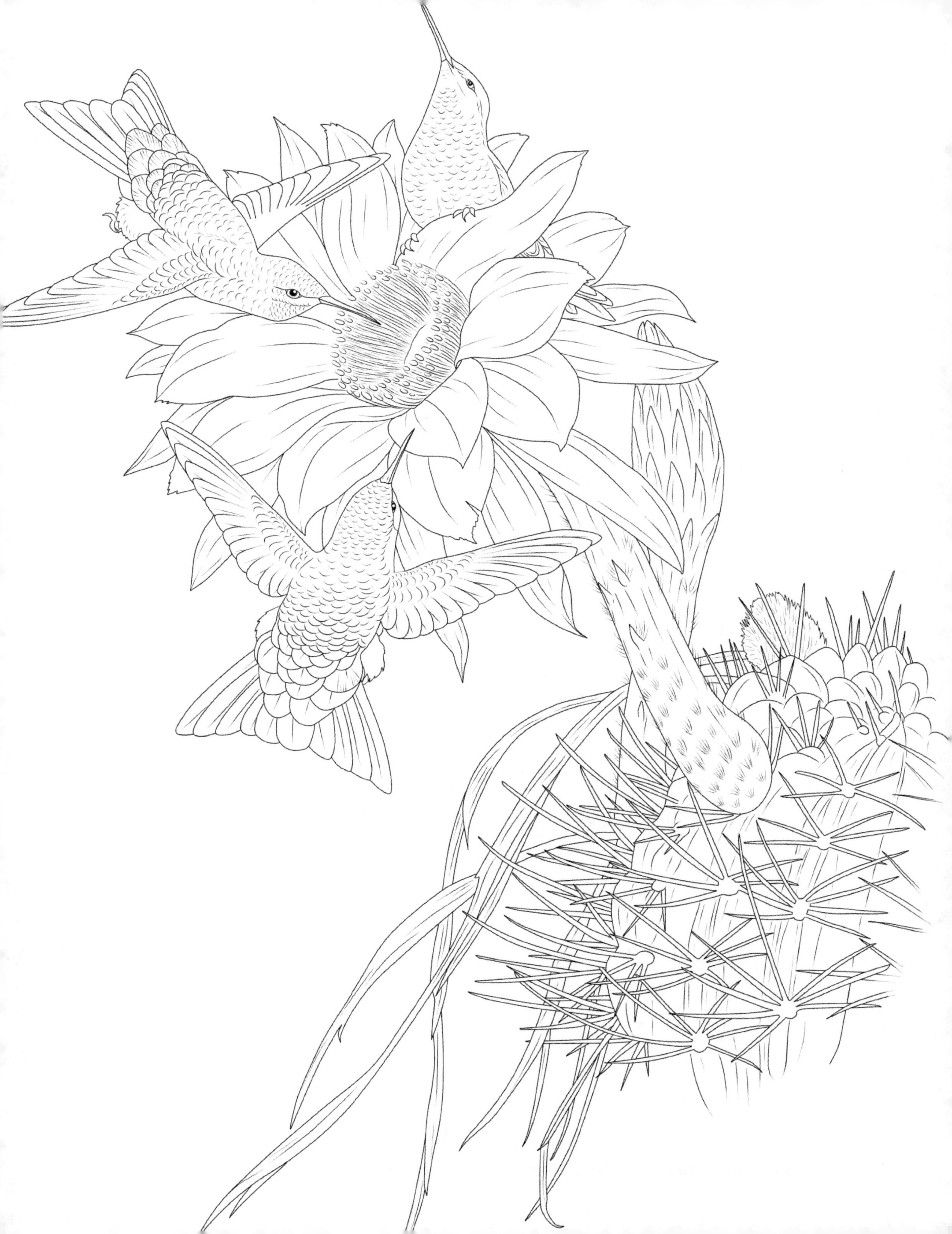

White-bellied Emerald Hummingbird (Thaumatias albiventris)

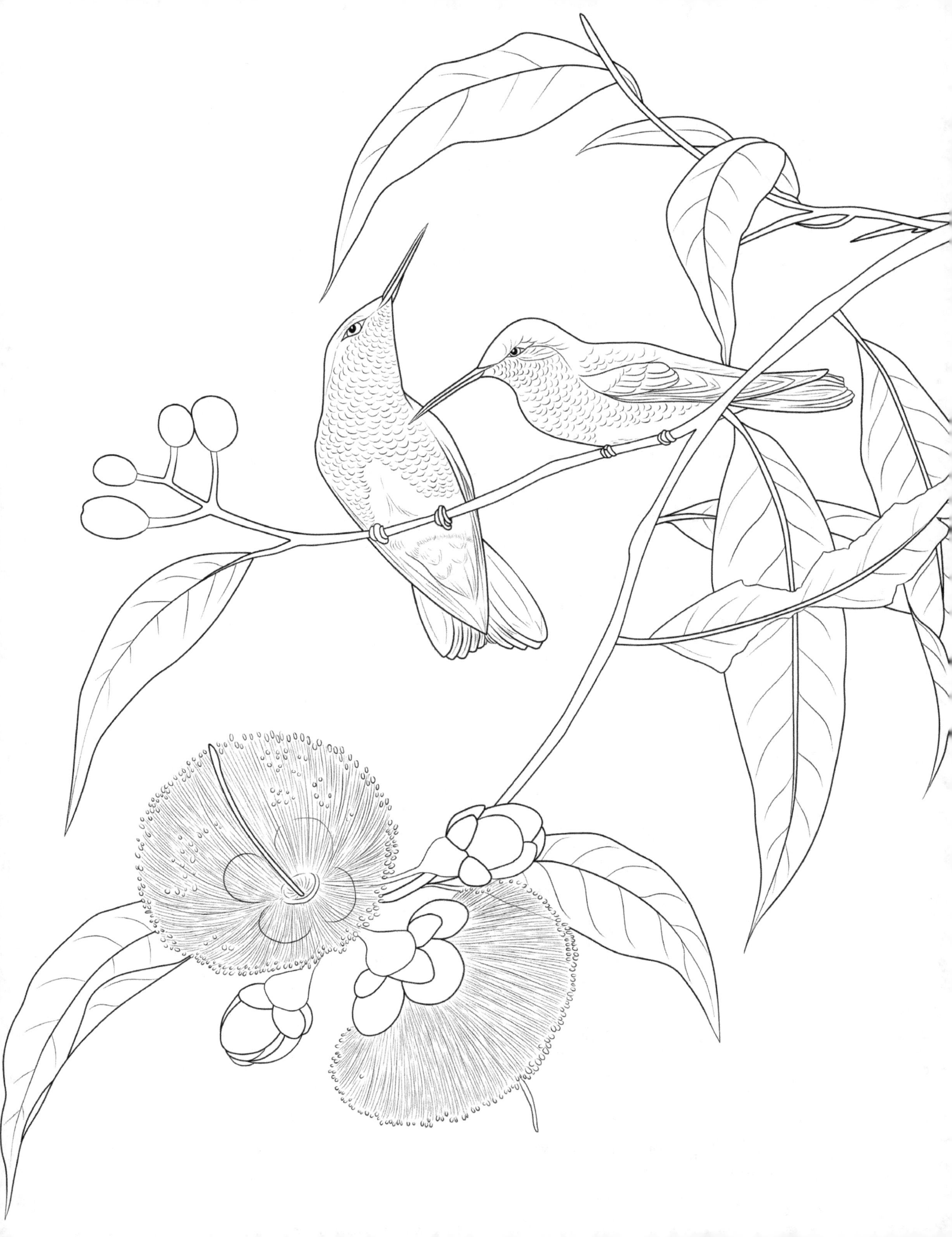

Empress Hummingbird (Eugenia imperatrix)
flower: Angel's Trumpet (Datura)

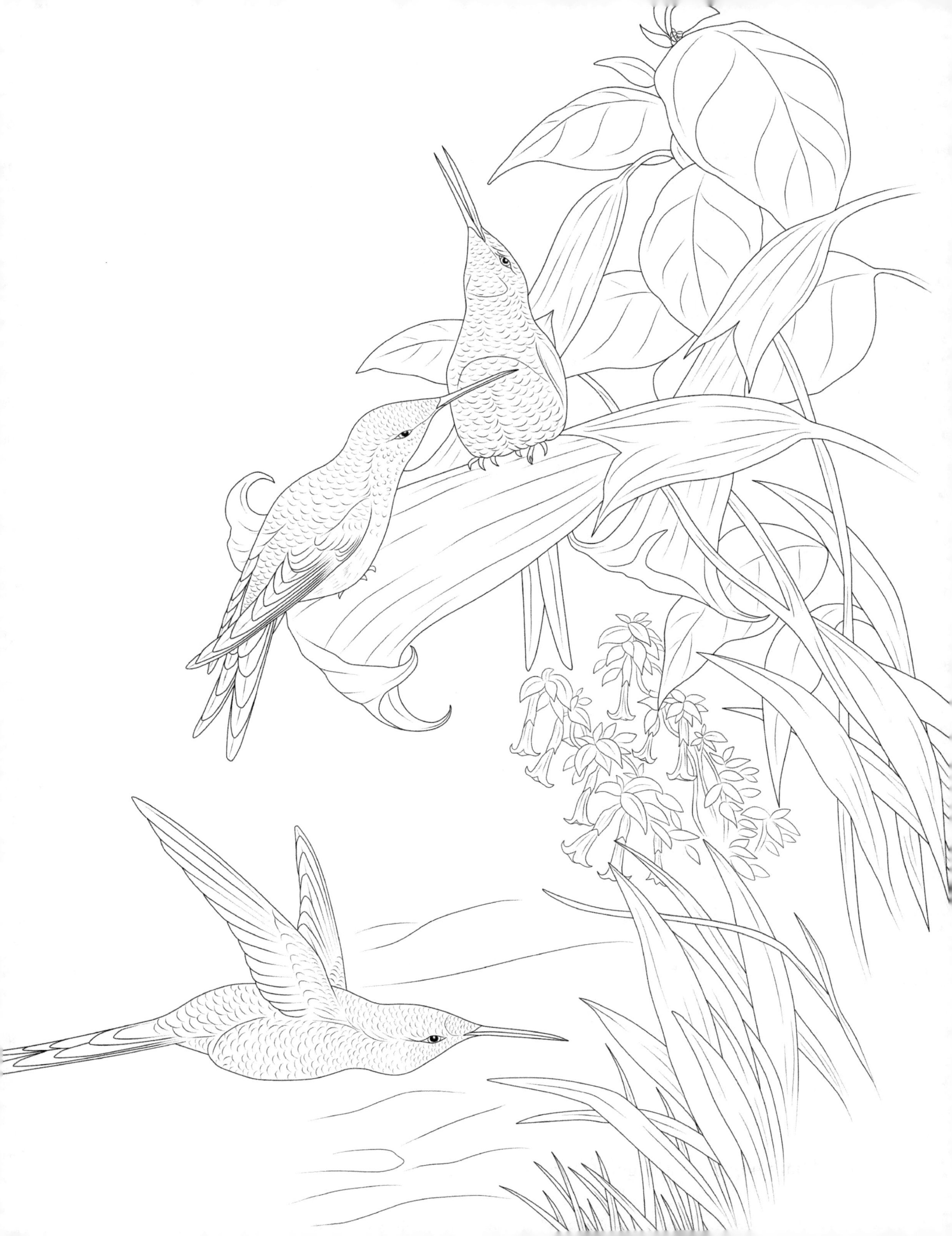

Pale-tailed Barbthroat Hummingbird (Threnetes leucurus)

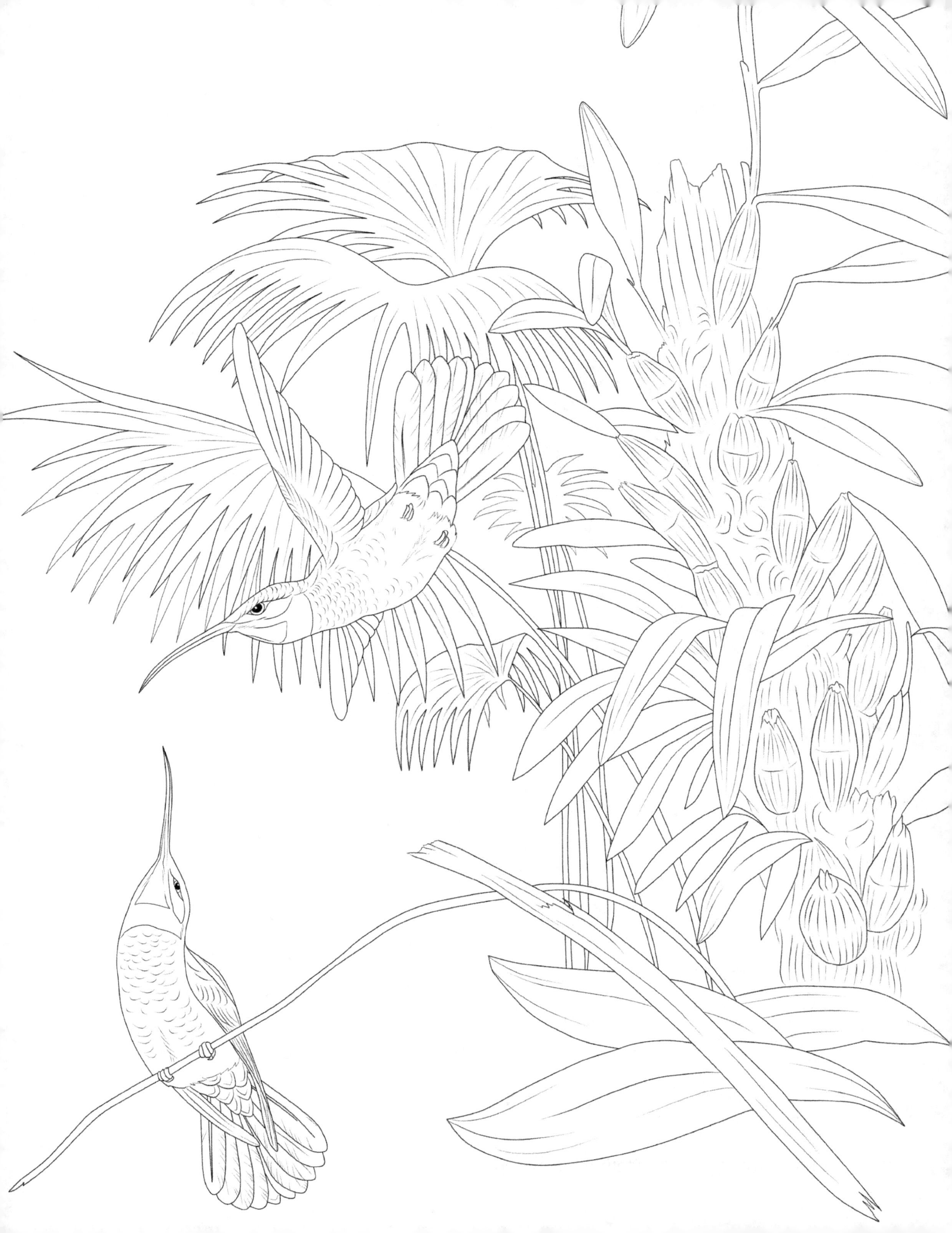

Pallid Hermit Hummingbird (Phaethornis anthophilus)

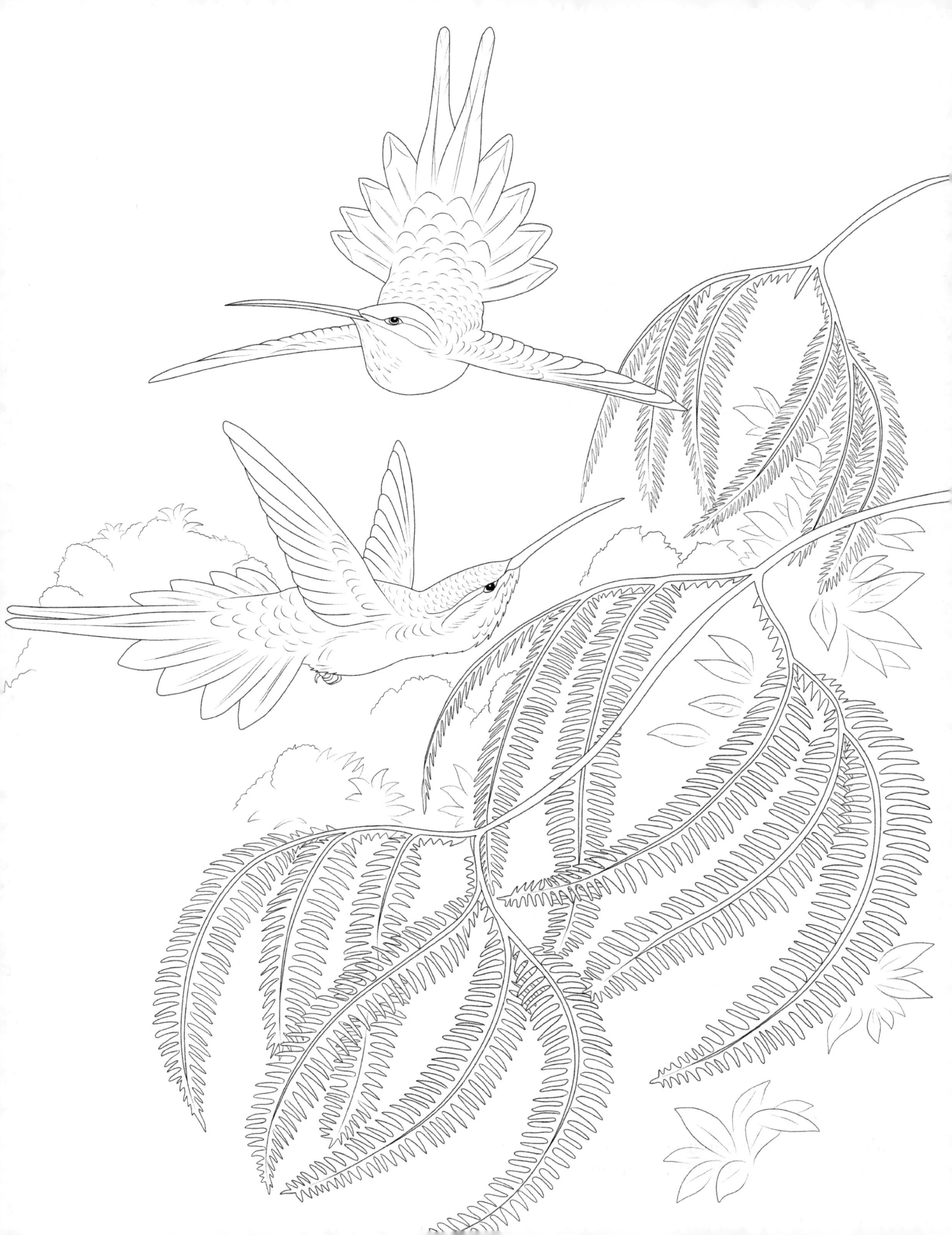

Sallé's Hermit Hummingbird (Phaethornis augusti)
flower: Stemonacanthus macrophyllus

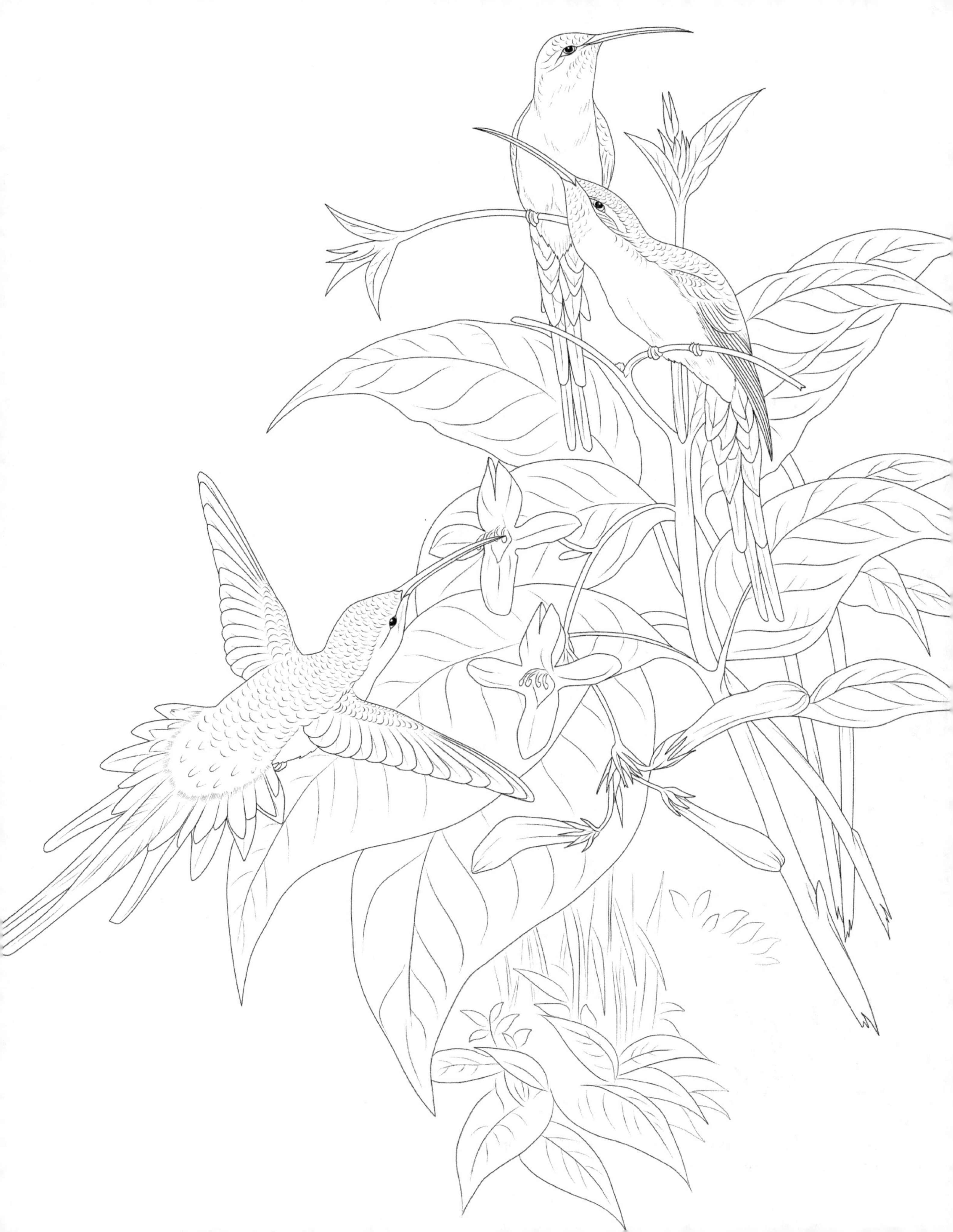

Buff-breasted Leucippus Hummingbird (Leucippus fallax)
flower: Dictyanthus pavonii

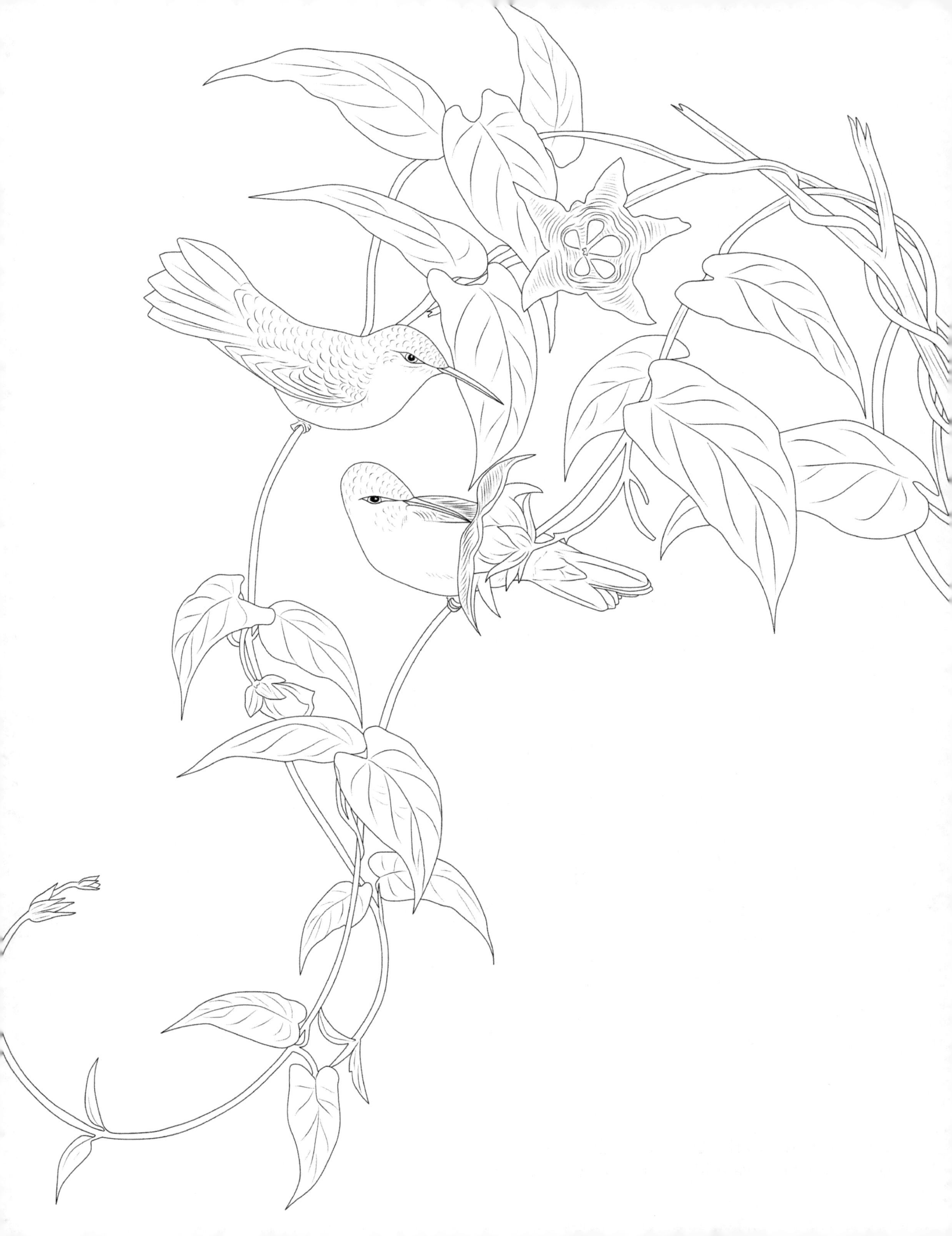

Purple-throated Carib (*Eulampis jugularis*)
flower: Amazon Waterlily (*Nymphaea amazonum*)

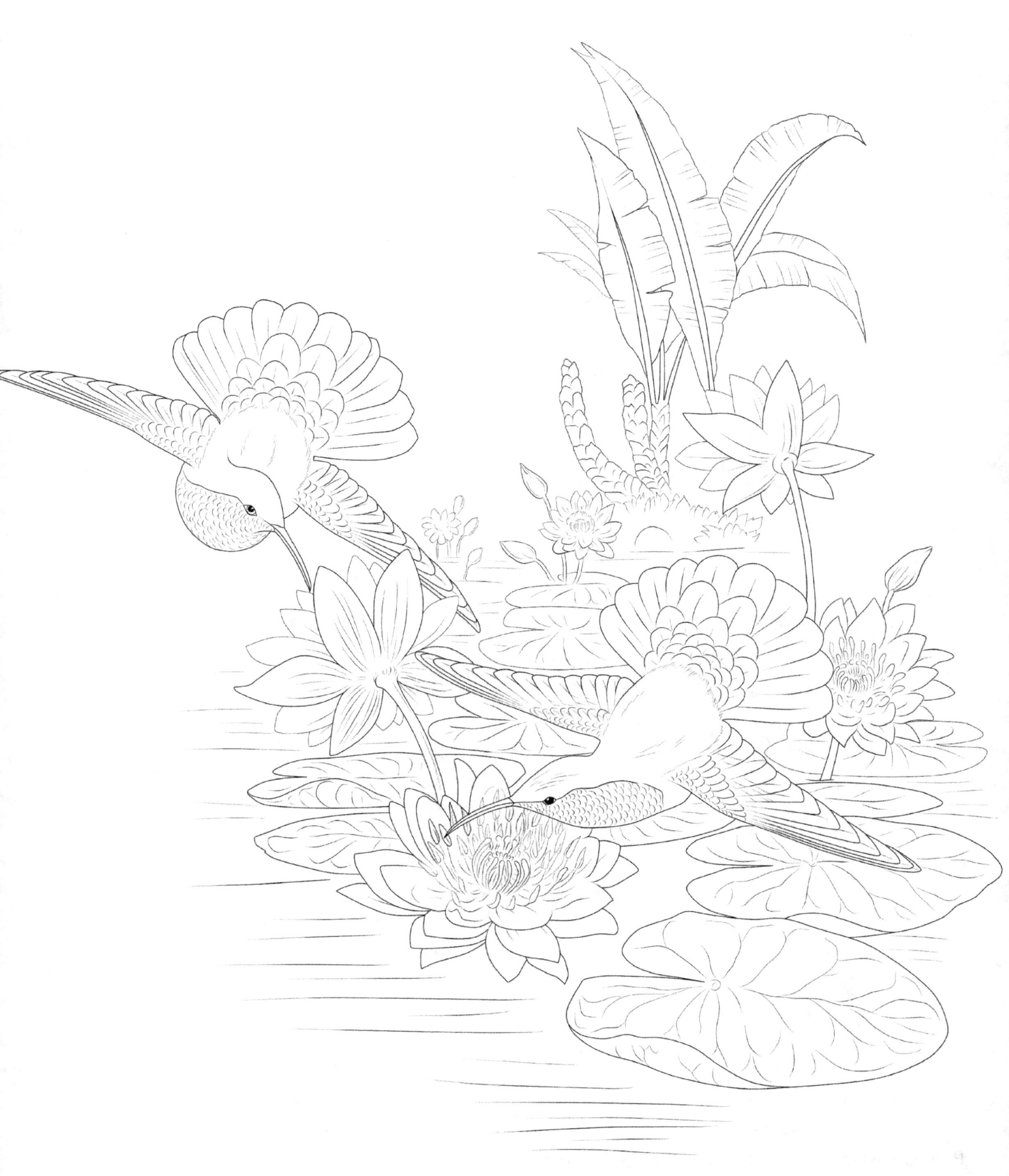

Prevost's Mango Hummingbird (Lampornis prevosti)
flower: Lacepedea insignia

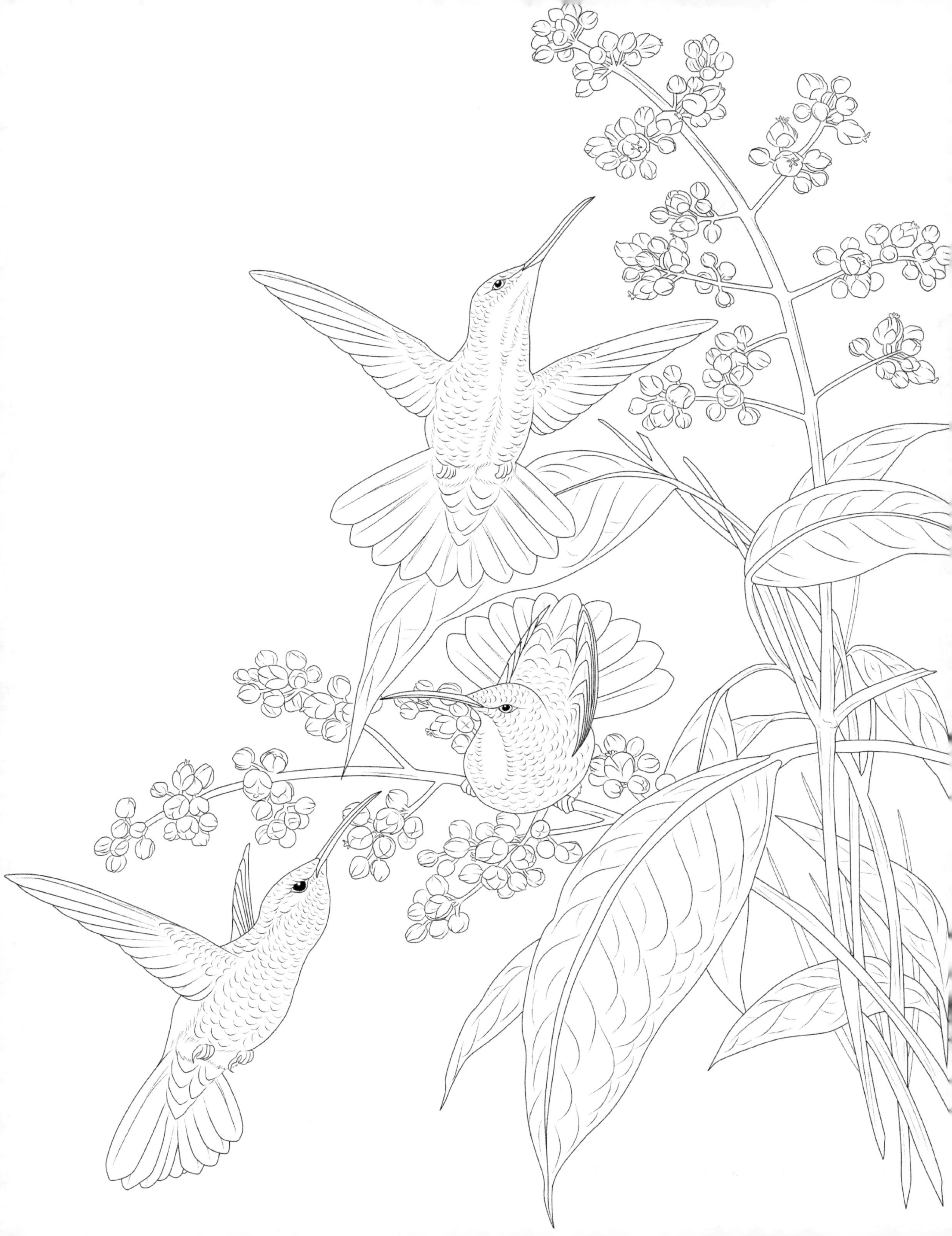

Fiery Topaz Hummingbird (Topaza pyra)

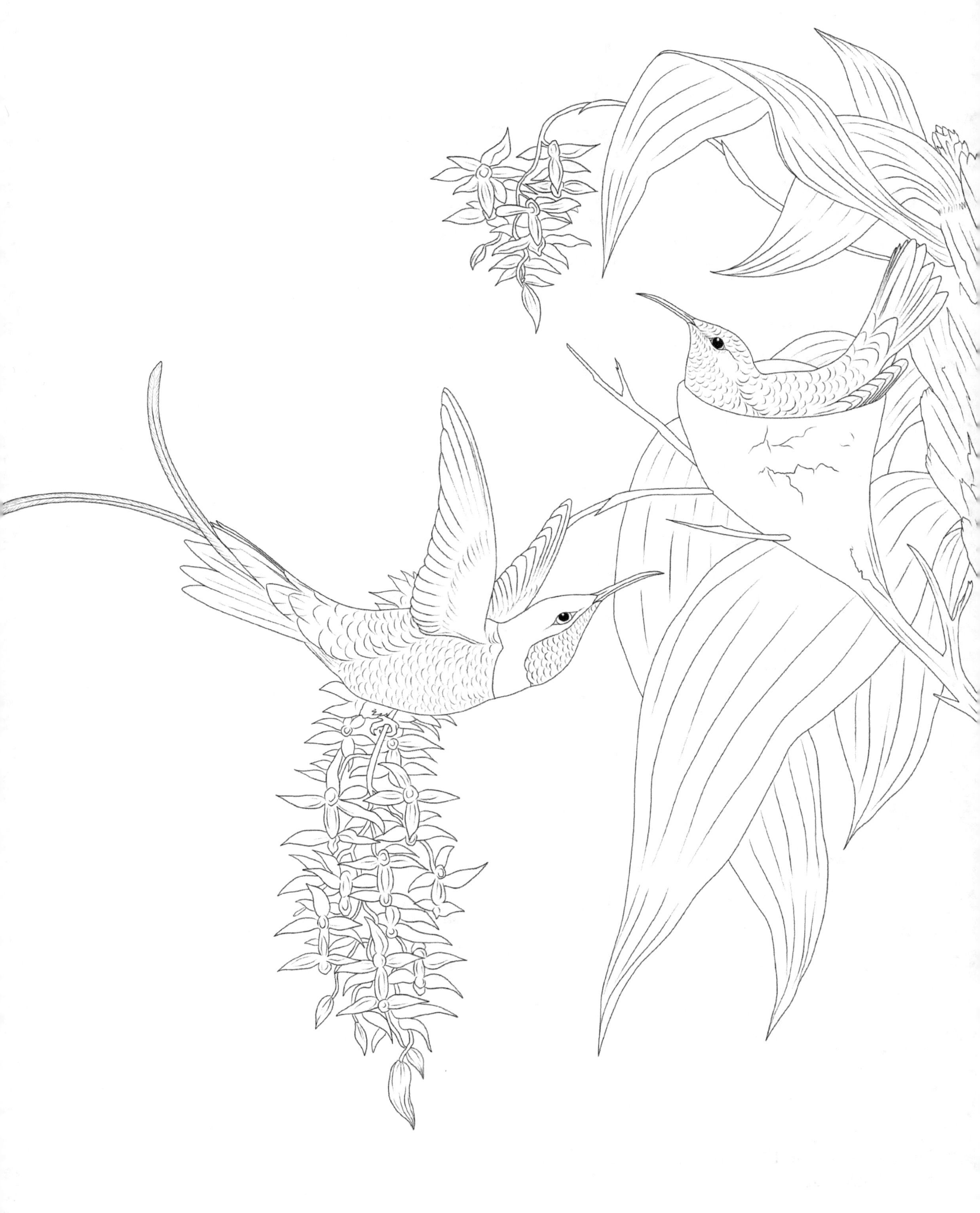

Jameson's Brilliant Hummingbird (Heliodoxa jamesoni)
flower: Orange Trumpetbush (Tecoma fulva)

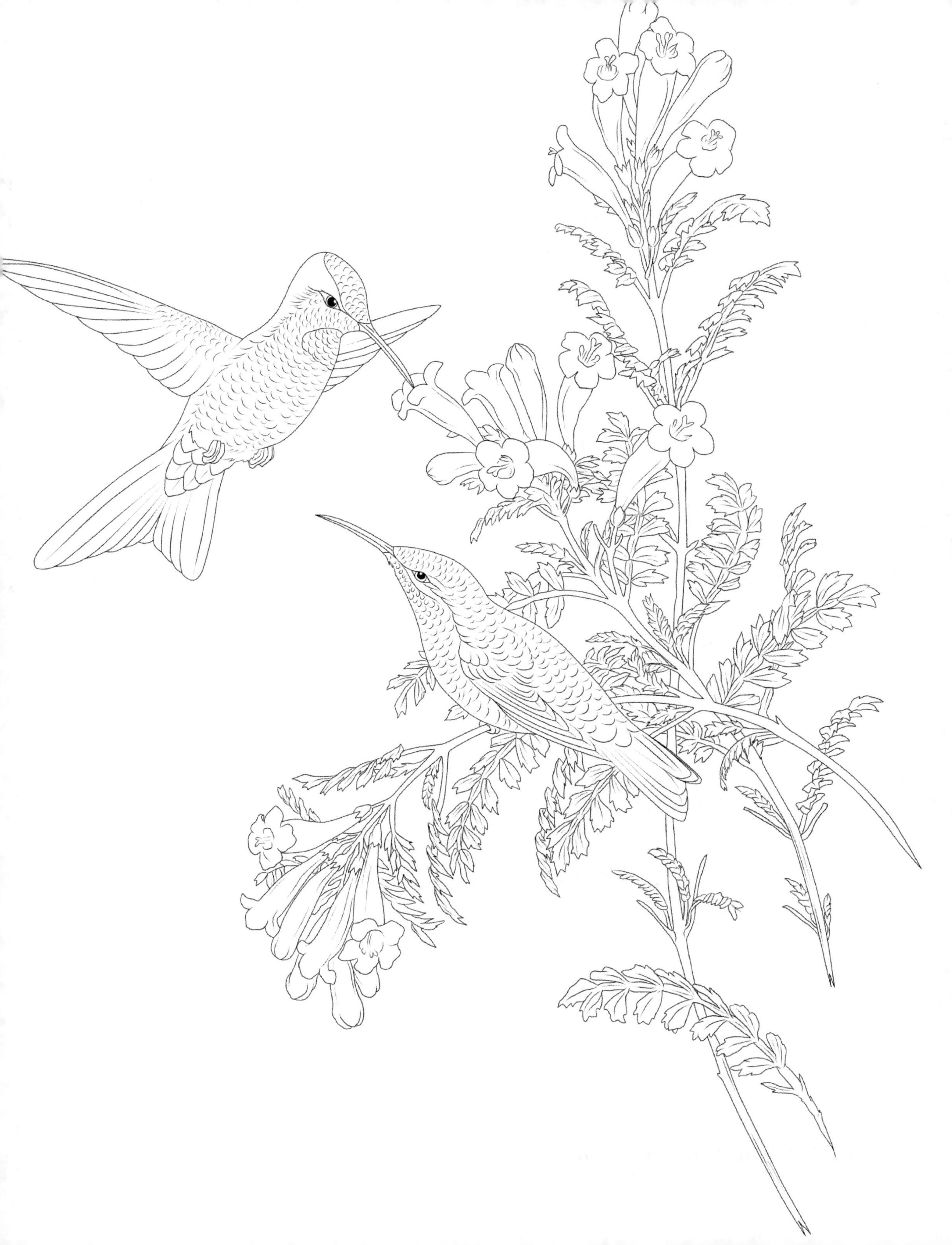

Leadbeater's Brilliant (Heliodoxa leadbeateri)
flower: Trichopilia Suavis Orchid

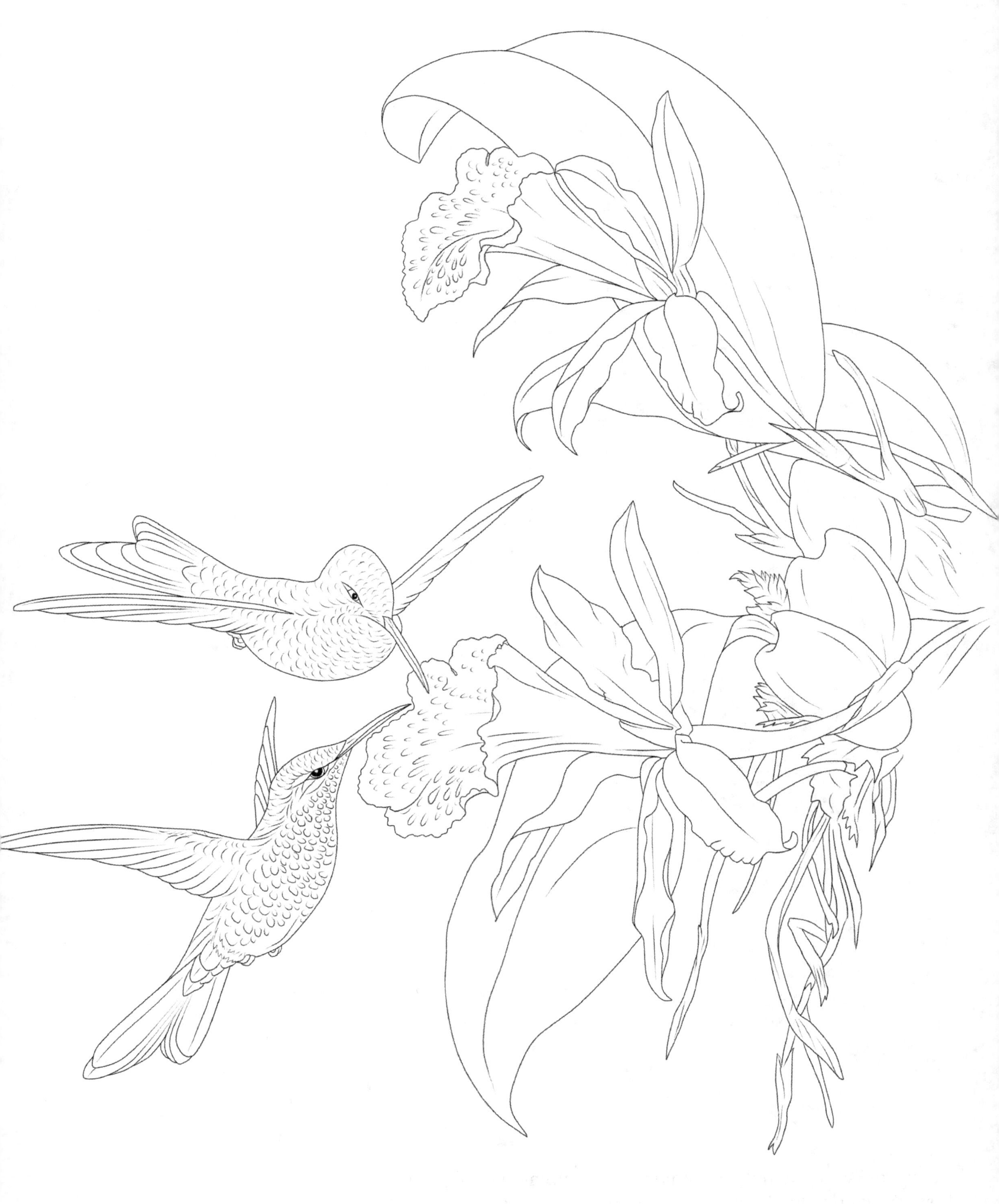

Refulgent Wood-nymph Hummingbird (Thalurania refulgens)
flower: Mandevilla (Dipladenia splendins)

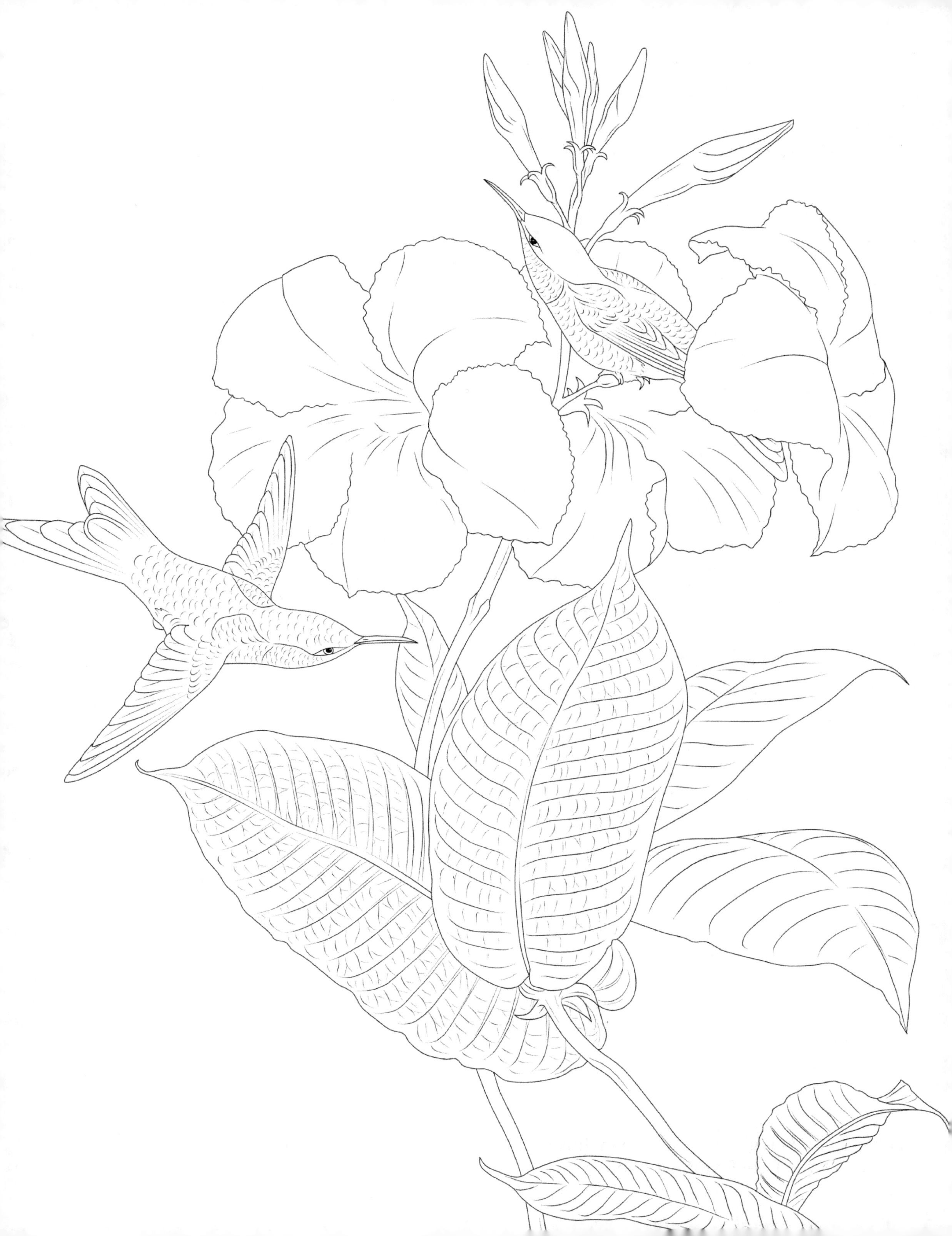

Jacobin Hummingbird (Florisuga mellivora)
flower: Flame Tree (Erythrina umbrosa)

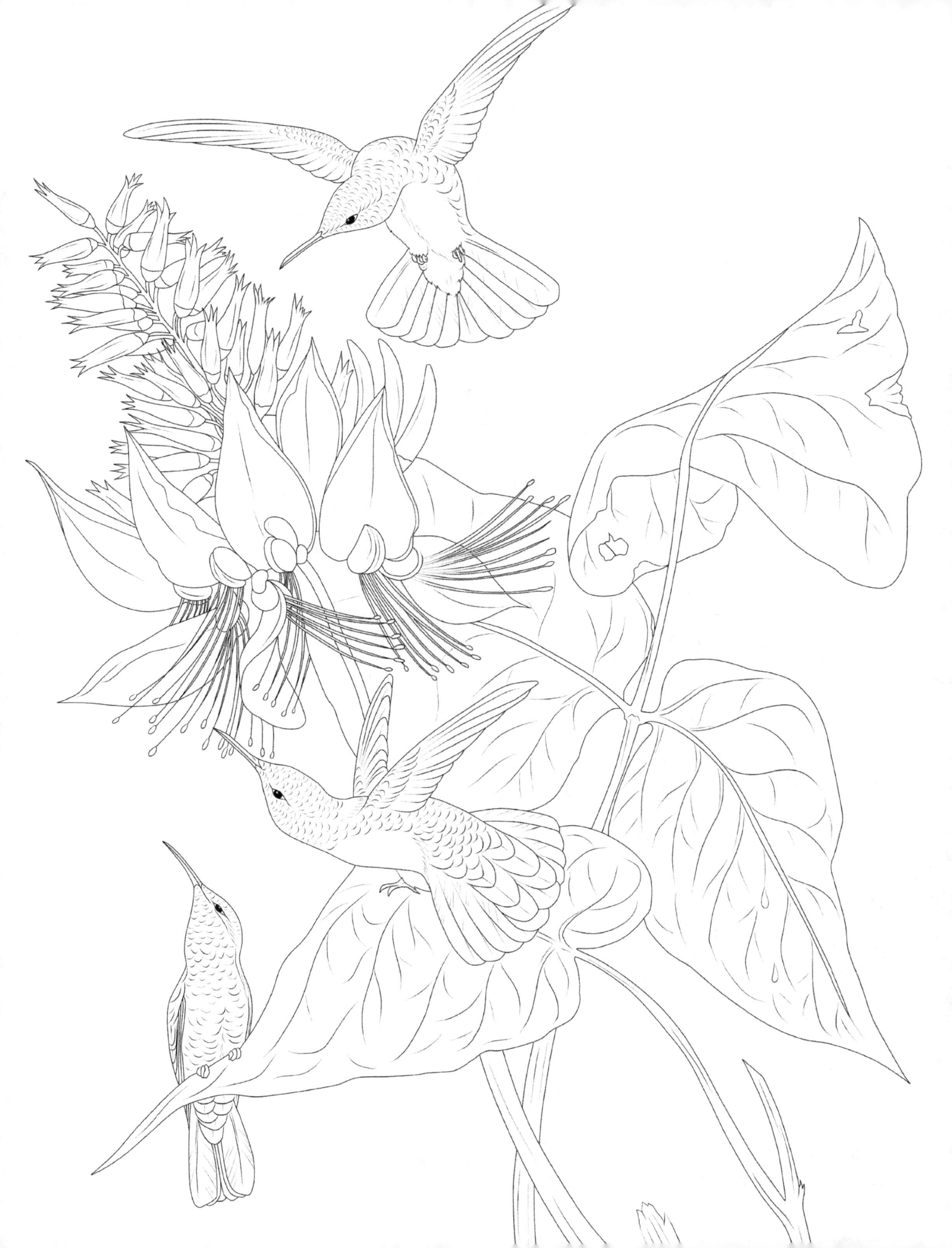

Marvelous Spatuletail Hummingbird (Loddigesia mirabilis)
flower: Hohenberg Bromeliad (Aechmea mertensii)

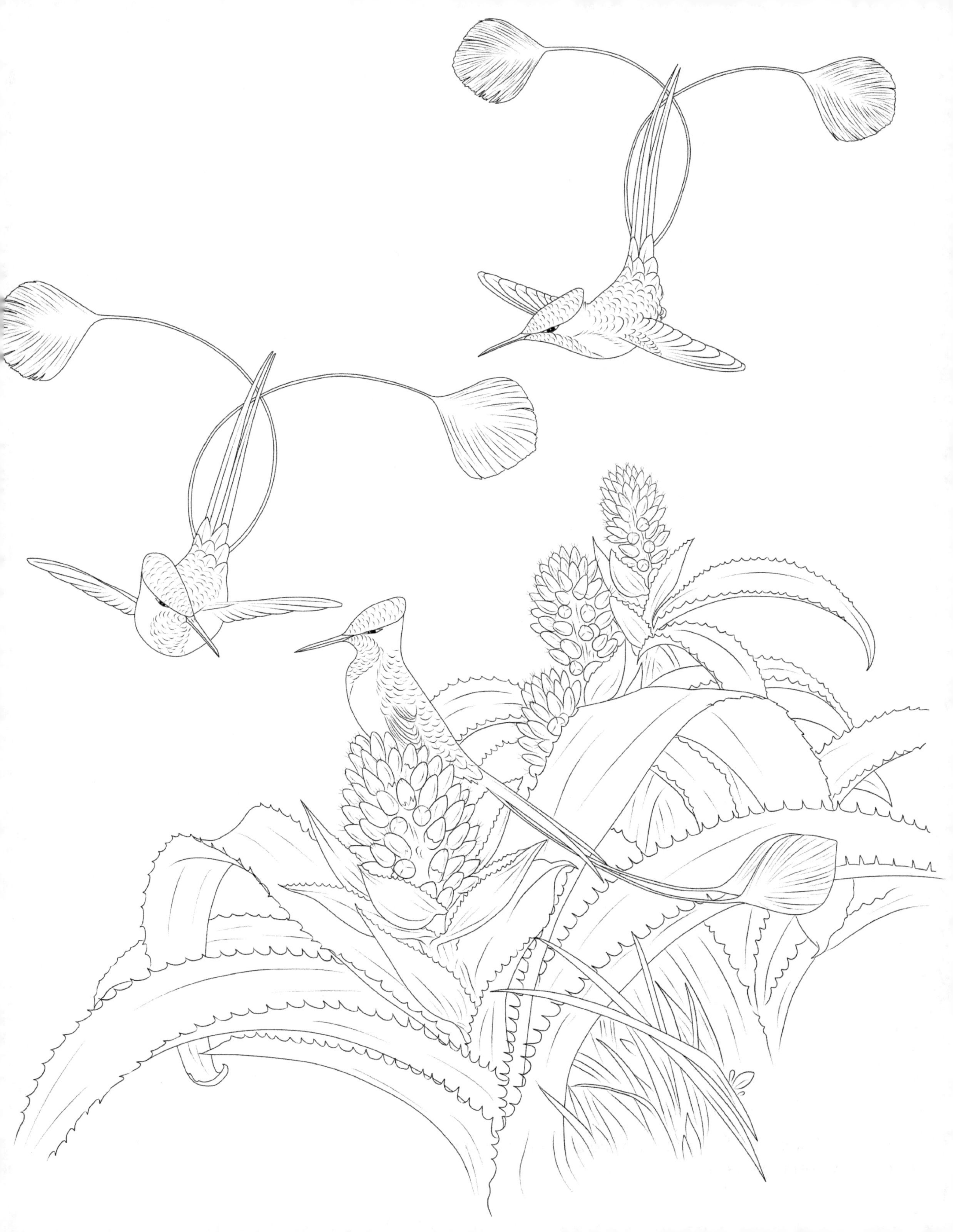

Bolivian Violet-ear Hummingbird (Petasophora iolata)
flower: Vriesia glaucophylla

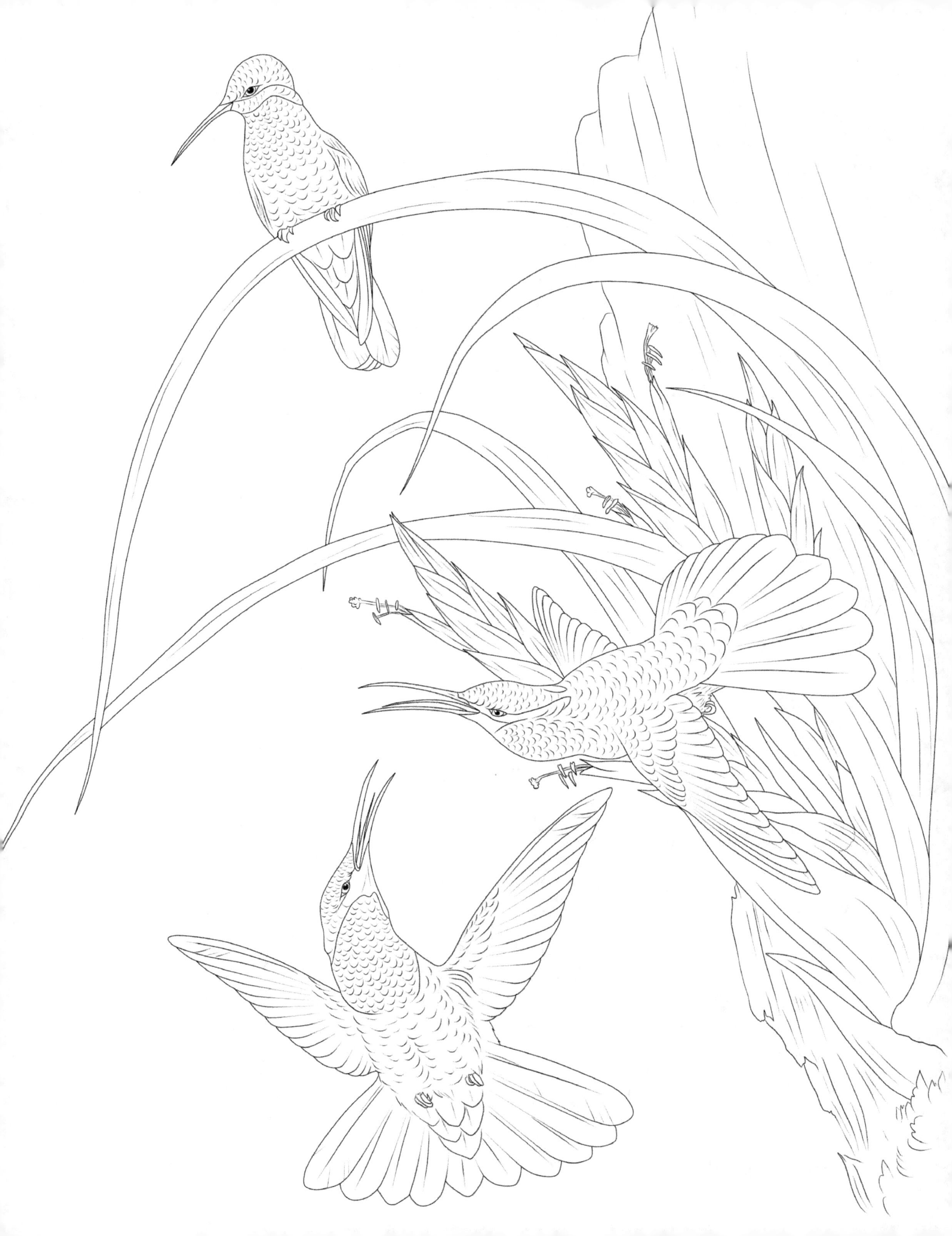

Rainbow Hummingbird (Diphogena iris)

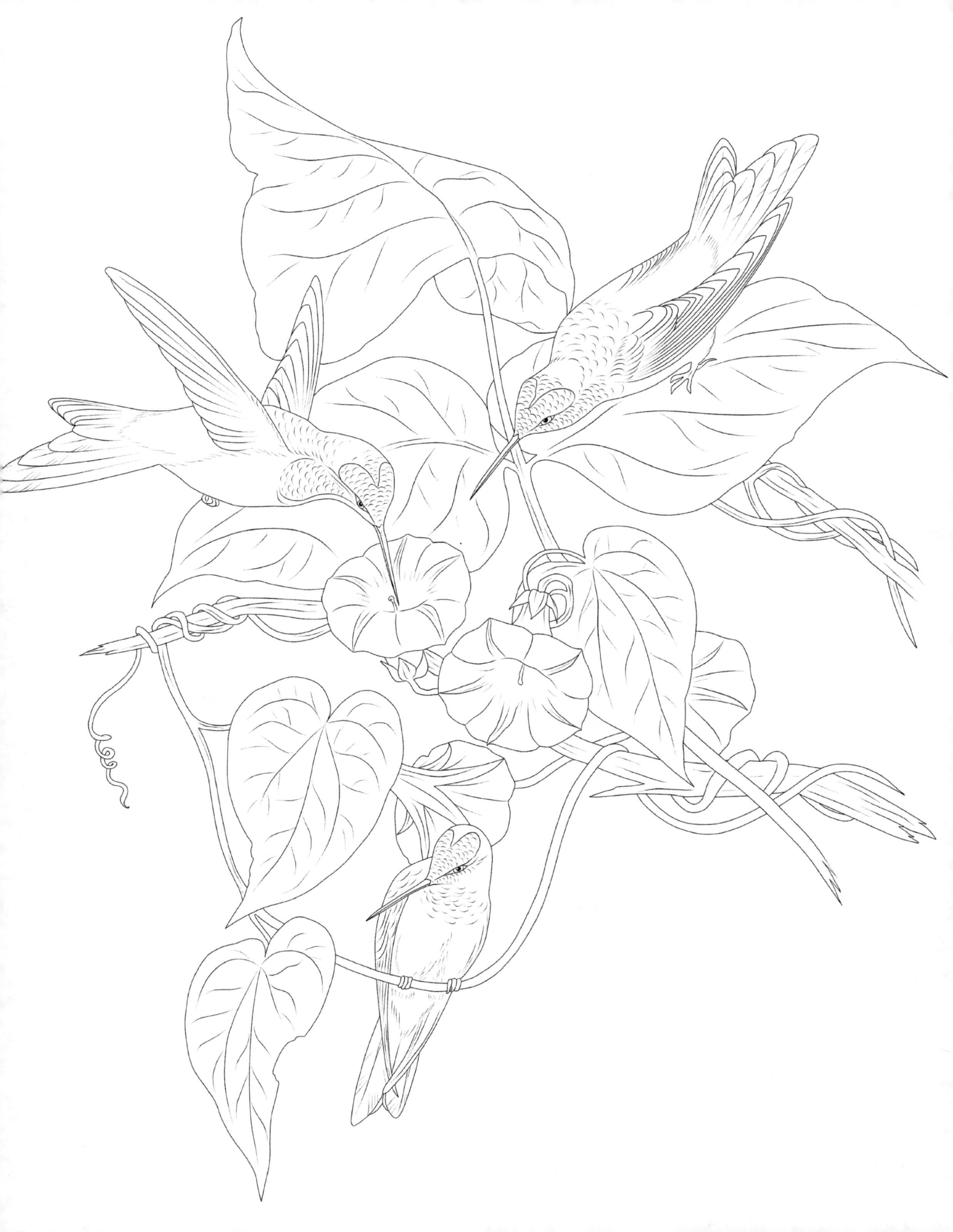

Guiana Violet-ear Hummingbird (Petasophora germana)

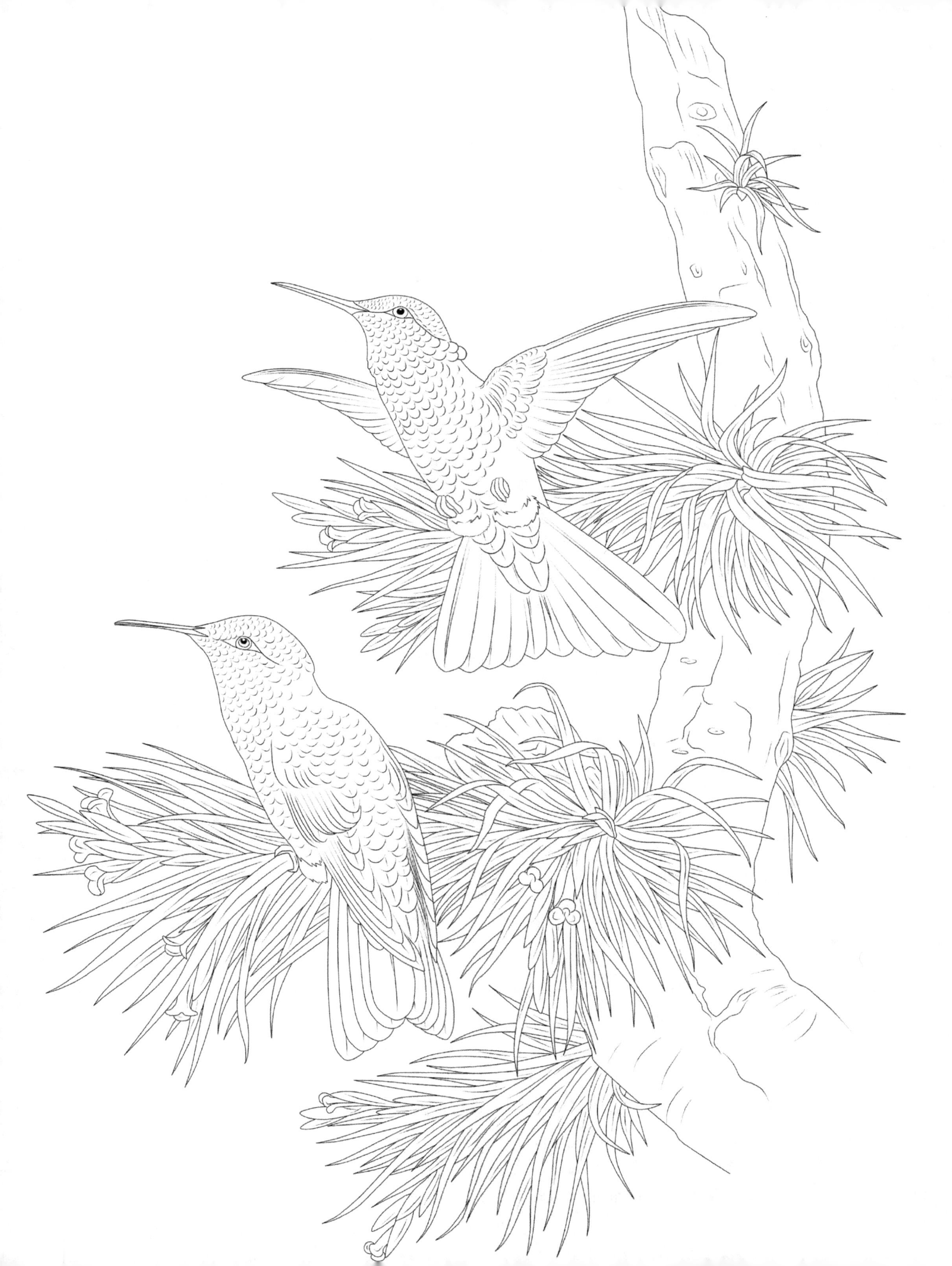

Lerch's Sapphire Hummingbird (Timolia lerchi)

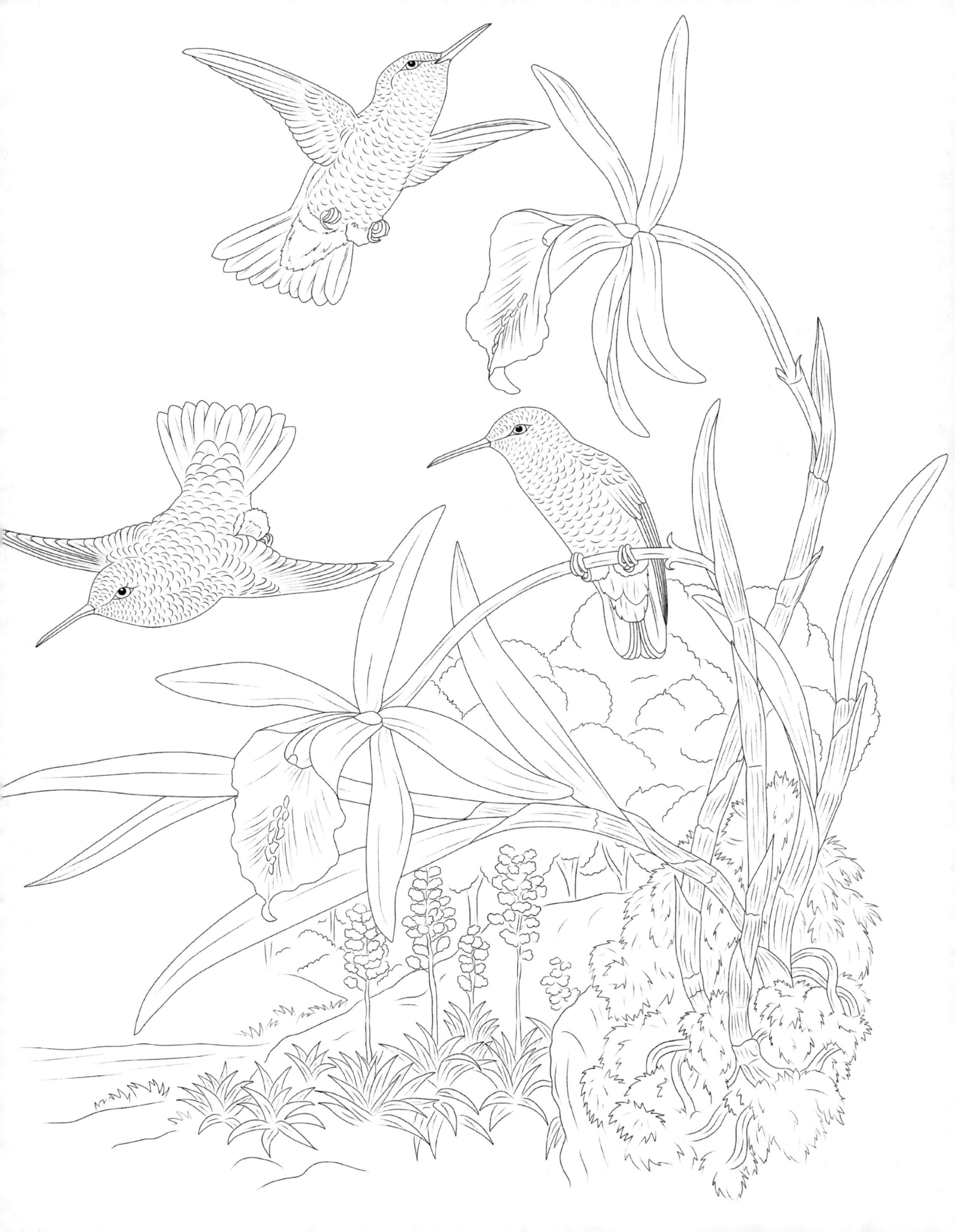

Sword-bill Hummingbird (Docimastes ensiferus)
flower: Scarlet Trumpet Flower (Brugmansia sanguinea)

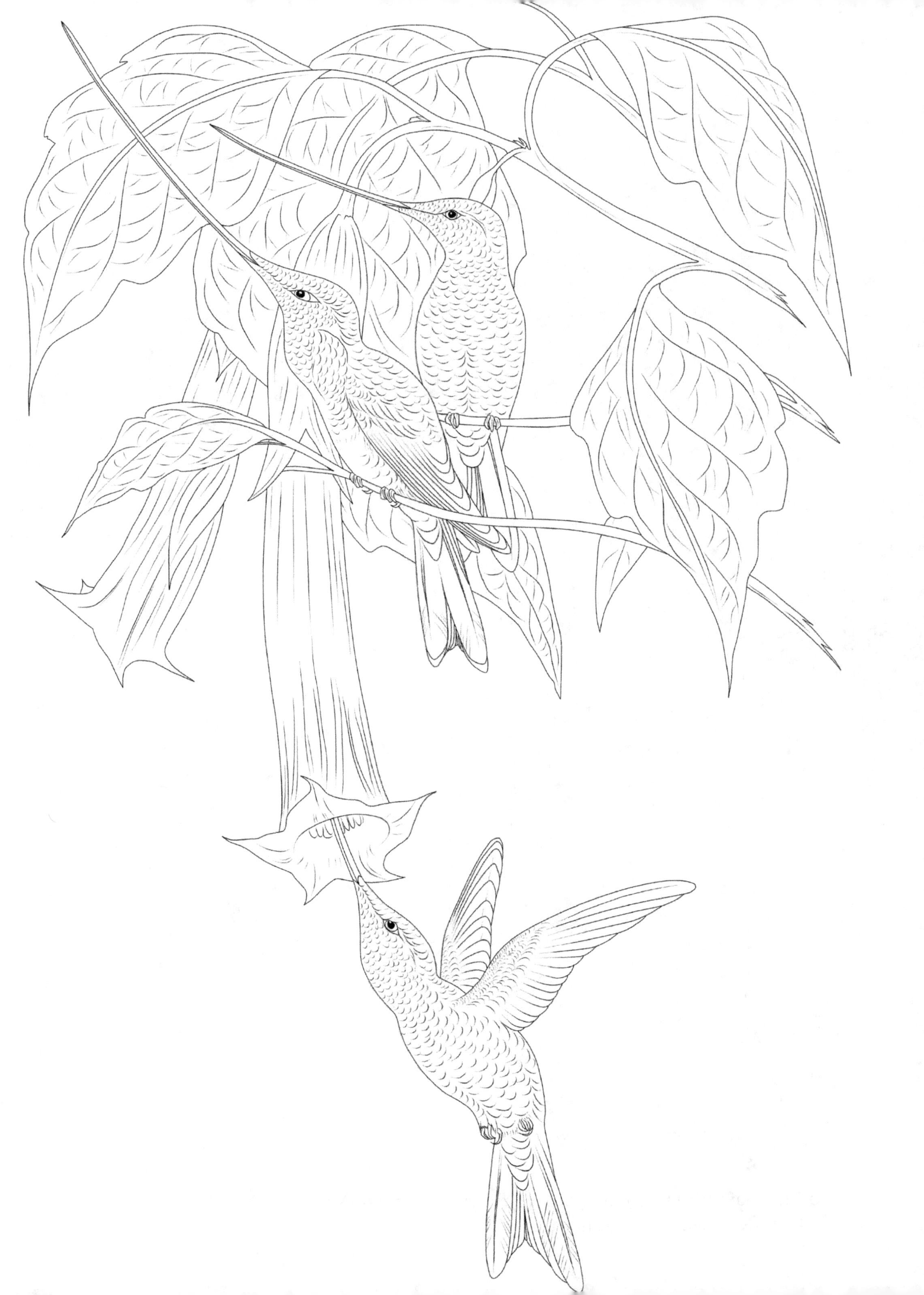

Green and Blue Sapphire Hummingbird (Hylonympha macrocerca)
flower: Chilean Bellfower (Lepageria rosea)

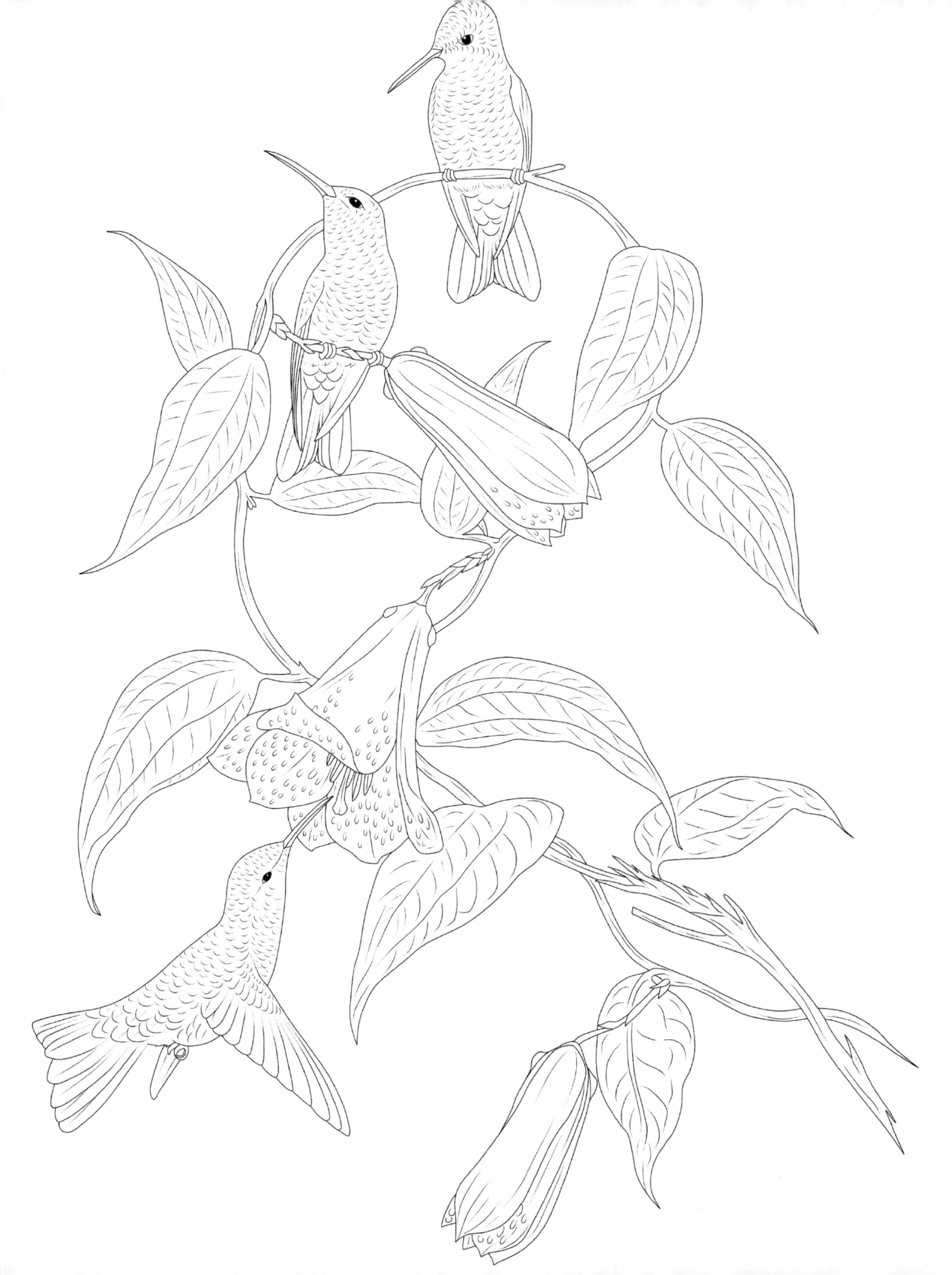

Great Fork-tailed Hummingbird (Eucephala smaragdo-caerulea)
flower: Chilean Bellflower (Lepageria rosea)

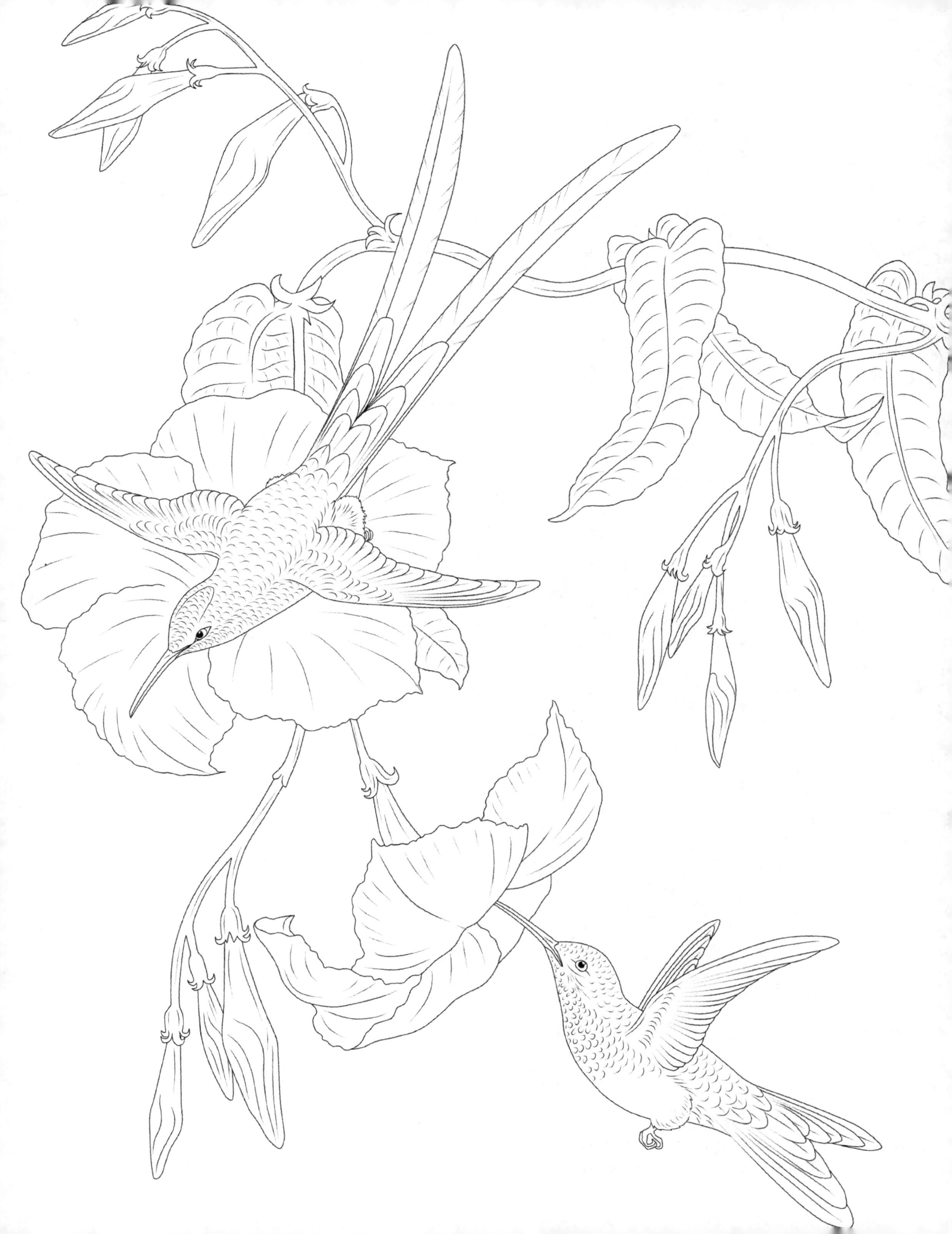

St. Domingo Hummingbird (Sporadinus elegans)
flower: Morning Glory (Pharbitis cathartica)

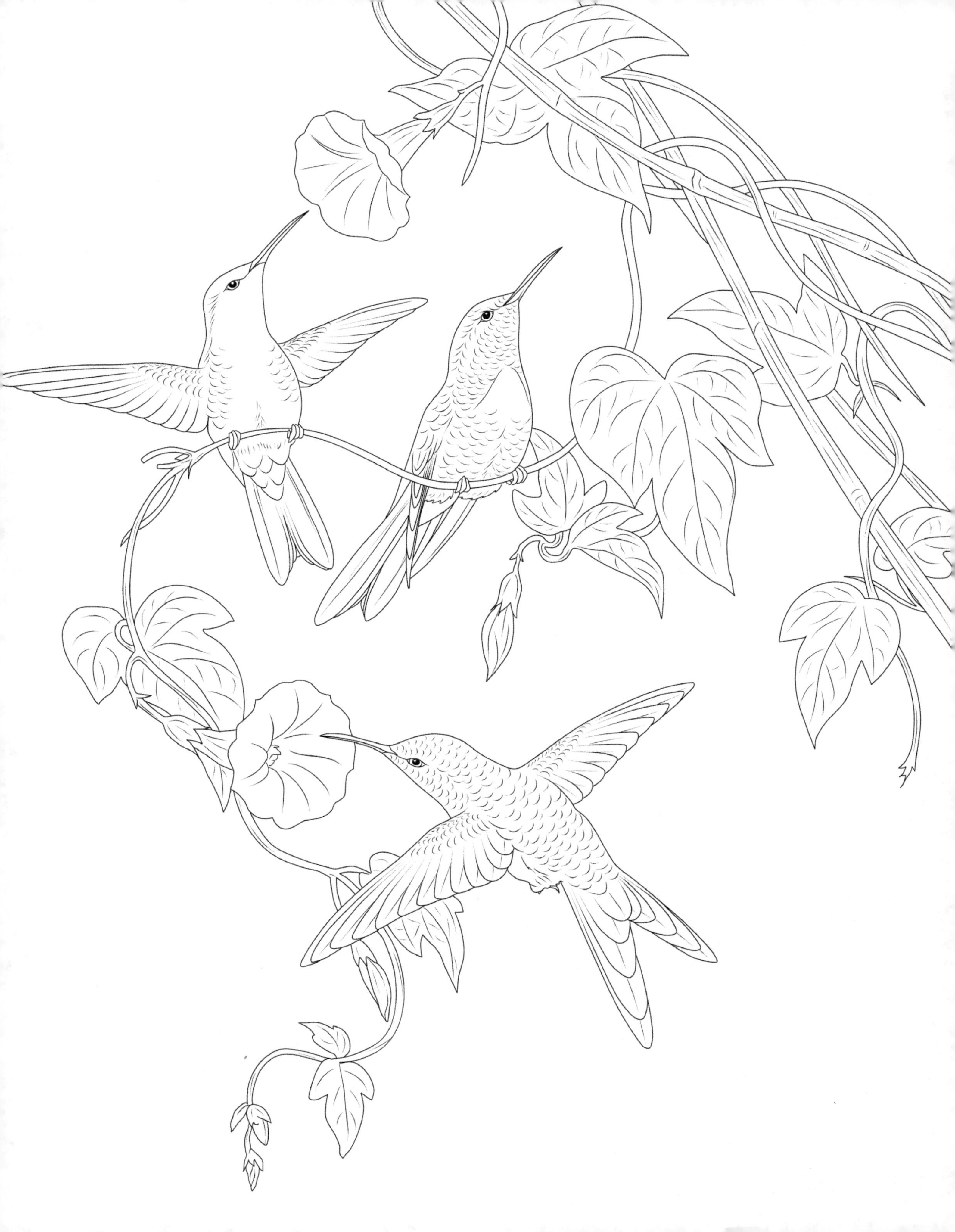